VIOLENCE AGAINST WOMEN

VIOLENCE AGAINST WOMEN

L. P. GORDON (EDITOR)

Novinka Books
New York

Senior Editors: Susan Boriotti and Donna Dennis
Coordinating Editor: Tatiana Shohov
Office Manager: Annette Hellinger
Graphics: Wanda Serrano
Editorial Production: Vladimir Klestov, Matthew Kozlowski and Maya Columbus
Circulation: Ave Maria Gonzalez, Vera Popovic, Luis Aviles, Raymond Davis,
Melissa Diaz and Jeannie Pappas
Marketing: Cathy DeGregory

Library of Congress Cataloging-in-Publication Data

Violence against Women / L.P. Gordon (editor).
    p. cm.
  Includes bibliographical references and index.
  ISBN: 1-59033-455-8.
    1. Women—Crimes against—United States. 2. Women—Violence against—
United States. 3. Women—Legal status, laws, etc.—United States. 4. Victims of
crimes—Legal status, laws, etc.—United States. I. Gordon, L.P.

HV6250.4.W65 V525 2002
362.88'082—dc21

                                                                  2002033700

Copyright © 2002 by Novinka Books, An Imprint of
                  Nova Science Publishers, Inc.
                  400 Oser Ave, Suite 1600
                  Hauppauge, New York 11788-3619
                  Tele. 631-231-7269   Fax 631-231-8175
                  e-mail: Novascience@earthlink.net
                  Web Site: http://www.novapublishers.com

Printed in the United States of America

CONTENTS

PREFACE

Violent attacks on women occur in almost every area of their daily lives. Women are assaulted in their homes, on the streets, in the workplace, at schools and on campuses. Victims must often face the emotional trauma of both physical and sexual abuse from the attack, the fear that future assaults will occur, and concerns confidentiality and confronting the offender within the criminal justice system.

Although fear of crime is widespread in the United States, polls indicate that more than twice as many women as men are afraid to walk at night near their homes. Though sexual assault is one of the most obvious examples of violence against women, such violence can take other forms. For example, media accounts have recently highlighted crime since such as stalking, domestic battery, and the growth in assaults against women by offenders unknown to them.

Gender-based discrimination, harassment, and violence against women in the home, workplace, and society at large are continuing topics of legislative and judicial concern. Legal doctrines condemning the extortion of sexual favors as a condition of employment or job advancement, and other sexually offensive workplace behaviors resulting in a "hostile environment," have evolved from judicial decisions under Title VII of the 1964 Civil Rights Act and related federal laws. The earlier judicial focus on economic detriment or quid pro quo harassment—making submission to sexual demands a condition to job benefits—has largely given way to Title VII claims alleging harassment that creates an "intimidating, hostile, or offensive environment." In 1994, Congress broke new legal ground by creating a civil rights cause of action for victims of "crimes of violence motivated by gender." The new law also made it a federal offense to travel interstate with the intent to "injure, harass, or intimidate" a spouse, causing bodily harm to the spouse by a crime of violence.

Violent attacks on women occur in almost every area of daily life. Victims often face trauma physically, emotionally and sexually. The processing of complaints by female victims of violence within the criminal justice system varies according to crime type and official attitudes. This book details federal concerns and possible solutions to the widespread problem of the perpetration of violence on women.

Chapter 1

VIOLENCE AGAINST WOMEN: AN OVERVIEW

Suzanne Cavanagh, Leslie Gladstone and David Teasley

SUMMARY

One of the most important aspects of the victim-offender relationship in violent crimes against women concerns the frequency in which women are attacked by intimates. For example, contrary to the accepted stereotype that women are most in danger of rape by strangers, a national study found that only 22 percent of all cases fit this category.

The processing of complaints by female victims of violence to within the criminal justice system may vary according to the nature of the crime, the type of complaint, and responses of criminal justice officials. First, the victim must determine whether or not to report to the crime. Law enforcement officials on the scene decide if the crime warrants arresting the offender. Judges, prosecutors, and defense attorneys must agree upon the charge and the disposition of the case.

The range of solutions currently offered regarding control of crime generally apply equally to gender-based crime, and tend to produce two kinds of recommendations. Some advocates proposed tougher prison sentences with the goal of removing wrongdoers from the streets for longer periods of time and, furthermore, of demonstrating that these crimes will be severely punished. Stronger Federal laws, although applying to only a limited number of situations where Federal jurisdiction is primary, also tended to set a standard for those State and local jurisdictions with weaker statutes and to provide a model for reform. Other advocates of change to believe that, while legal reforms are needed, they should be augmented by programs to activate community resources, involving the public, law enforcement, and the courts in changing attitudes concerning the problem of public safety for women.

INTRODUCTION

Violent attacks on women occur in almost every area of their daily lives. Women are assaulted in their houses, on the streets, in the workplace, and schools, and on campuses. Victims often must face the emotional trauma of both physical and sexual abuse from the attack, the fear that future assaults will occur, and their concerns about confidentiality and confronting the offender within the criminal justice system.

Although fear of crime is widespread in the United States, pools indicate that more than twice as many women as men are afraid to walk at night near their homes,[1] illustrating the perceived vulnerability that tends to limit women's lives in many ways. According to recent Senate testimony, women's concerns regarding their personal safety tend to circumscribe basic economic, and social choices, not only in jobs, but in housing, education, community service, and recreation.[2] The costs of limitations imposed by gender-based violence, both on women personally and on society at large, are difficult to fully assess. In comments concerning violence against women, one expert testified that "it must be recognized that this is not a special-interest topic, but a national problem of serious proportions."[3]

The best documented category of violent crime against women is rape. During the hearings before the Senate Judiciary Committee, a spokesperson for the American Psychological Association presented evidence that one in

---

[1] Gallup Organization. Public Sees Crime Up Nationally. *Gallup Poll Monthly.* March 1992. p. 51-53 and ABC News. Crime in America. *ABC News/Day One Poll.* November 7, 1993.

[2] U.S. Congress. Senate. Committee on the Judiciary. *Violence Against Women: A Week in the Life of America. S. Print 102-118, 102d Cong., 2d Sess, October 1992.* Washington. U.s. Govt. Print. Off., p. 7.

[3] U.S. Congress. Senate. Committee on the Judiciary. *Women and Violence.* Hearings on Legislation to Reduce the Growing Problem of Violent Crime Against Women, 101st Congress, 2d Sess., Washington, U.S. Govt. Print. Off., 1991, p. 110. Hereafter referred to as Women and Violence.

five American women may be raped in her lifetime.[4] In the case of date rape, a study published by the National Victim Center in Arlington, Virginia, reported that 10 percent of the victims interviewed had been raped by their boyfriends or ex-boyfriends.[5]

Though sexual assault is one of the most obvious examples of violence against women, such violence can take other forms. Its impact was such that, in 1989, the Surgeon Captain General of the United States stated that violence was the most serious public health risk to adult American women.[6] Media accounts have recently highlighted crimes such as stalking,[7] domestic battery, and the growth in assaults against women by offenders unknown to them:

- In 1990, after five Orange County women were stopped and subsequently murdered by former husbands or boyfriend, California enacted the nation's first anti-stalking law[8],

- According to a 1992 report prepared by the majority staff of the Senate Judiciary Committee, each year more than 1.13 million women report being victims of domestic violence[9],

- In 1992, a U.S. Senators wife was attacked and dragged down the steps of her home and kidnapped by an armed assailant.[10]

This chapter provides statistics on rape, domestic battery, and other violence aimed at women. It offers an analysis of the issues involved in combatting gender-specific crimes, and arguments for and against recent

---

[4] *Ibid., p. 74.*

[5] Crime Victims Research Treatment Center and the National Victim Center. *Rape in America: A Report to the Nation.* Arlington, Virginia, April 23, 1992. p.4. Hereafter referred to as *Rape in America.*

[6] Staff Report, p.1.

[7] In 1990 California pass to the first State's anti-stalking law. Since then, 47 states have enacted such measures. Although anti-stalking statutes vary in their definition of stalking, most include the following characteristics among proscribed behaviors: harassment, lying-in-wait, non-consequential communication, and surveillance. See, U.S. Department of Justice. National Institute of Justice. Research Report. *Project to Develop a Model Anti-Stalking Code for States.* October 1993. pp. 13, 16-20.

[8] Resnick, Rosalind. States Enact 'Stalking' Laws. *National Law Journal*, vol. 14, May 11, 1992. p. 27.

[9] U.S. Congress. Senate. Committee on the Judiciary. *Violence Against Women: A Week in the Life of America.* Prepared by the Majority Staff of the Committee. Washington, D.C. October 1992. p. ix. Hereafter referred to as Staff Report.

[10] Foerstel, Karen. Conrad, Wife Recuperating From Night of Crime Horror. *Roll Call,* January 6, 1992. p. 3.

efforts by policymakers to address the problem of violence against women. Also, it presents a discussion of Federal prevention initiatives and efforts to reduce such activities.

THE DIMENSIONS OF VIOLENCE

Statistics

Interestingly, statistics on crimes of violence against women document a personal safety problem that some believe may seriously limit the ability of women to function fully in American society. Data measuring violence against women are insufficient to provide an accurate picture of the full extent of this problem. For example, statistics exist for the crime of rape, and to a lesser extent for domestic battery, but little information has been compiled on crimes such as stalking.

Rape

Statistics on rape may vary according to the definition of the offense and the type of methodology used in collecting and presenting the data. For example, but two official measures of crime in the United States, the FBI's Uniform Crime Reports (UCR) and the Bureau of Justice Statistics' National Crime Victimization Survey (NCVS), defining the rate as the coronal knowledge of a victim forcibly and against there will, but the UCR applies only to female victims while the NCVS includes homosexual rape. The two measures also use a different methodology to collect data. The UCR includes only instant sense reported to the police, while the NCVS surveys a national population age 12 or older.[11]

Rape statistics from these two data steps may be unreliable for other reasons: (1) female respondents defined rape for themselves without reference to any uniform criteria, (2) compilers of the data may fail to ask victims specific questions about the rape, and (row of 3) victims maybe reluctant to report the crime to interviewers.[12] *UCR* data, compiled from

---

[11] U.S. Department of Justice. Federal Bureau of Investigation. *Uniform Crime Reports for the United States 1992.* Washington, UJ.S. Govt. Print. Off., 1993. p. 23. Hereafter referred to as UCR. U.S. Department of Justice. Bureau of Justice Statistics. *Criminal Victimization in the United States, 1991.* Washington, December 1992, p. 156. Hereafter referred to as NCVS.

[12] According to the Bureau of Justice Statistics, "each victim defines the rape for herself. If she reports that she has been the victim of rape or attempted rape, she is not asked to explain what happened any further. On the other hand, no one in the survey is never asked directly

police reports, may not accurately measure the extent of the problem. For example, in a study of all the cases of female rape and attempted rape reported from 1973 to 1987, *NCVS* surveyors report that almost half (47 percent) of the victims did not report the crime to the police.[13] On the other hand, though cases of false report of rape to do exist, most law enforcement authorities estimate that only about five percent of all reported rapes may fall in this category.[14]

The *UCR* reported 109, 062 forcible rapes in 1992,a 2.3 – percent increase over the previous year. Between 1988 and 1992, the number of known rape offenses increased by 18 percent.[15] The *NCVS* estimated that, in 1991, there were 173,310 completed or attempted rapes of women age 12 or older, or 1.4 per 1000 women.[16]

Few studies have focused on trends in violence against women.[17] Statistics from *NCVS* for violent crimes against women, such as rape, robbery and assault, show a fairly steady rate of 21.8 per 1000 women age 12 and over in 1973 to 22.9 in 1991. Likewise, the rate of rapes reported by survey respondents showed a slight drop from 1.8 per 1000 women age 12 and over in 1973 to 1.4 in 1991.[18] At the same time, statistics on rape offenses *reported to police* nationwide provide evidence that the rate to per

---

if she has been raped. This response must come voluntarily in reply to a series of questions on bodily harm." (Beginning in the summer of 1993, all respondents to the survey are asked directly if they have been the victim of rape or attempted rape). Also, female respondents may be "reluctant report the event to the survey interviewer…. The exact amount of the understatement is impossible to ascertain." NCVS, p. 1.

Psychologists have criticized in the NCVS methodology on many of the same grounds, noting that: (1) family members or relatives may actually be present during the interview; (2) rape victims may be unlikely to disclose into the details to a stranger, especially if the interviewer it is male; and (3) respondents themselves decide whether or not a rape had actually occurred. For example, a woman victimized in the date rape may not perceive the incident as a crime. See testimony by Mary P. Koss, on behalf of the American Psychological Association That, women and violence as a crime. See testimony of Mary P. Koss, on behalf of the American Psychological Association, *Women and Violence*. pp. 38-42.

[13] Harlow, Caroline Wolf. *Female Victims of Violent Crime*. U.S. Department of Justice. Bureau of Justice cap Statistics. Washington, key. Seed., January 1991. p. 9. Hereafter referred to as *Female Victims of Violent Crime*. By 1991, *NCSV* surveyors reported that 41 percent of the victims did not report the crime to the police. *NCVS*, p. 8.

[14] Fairstein, Linda A. *Sexual Violence: Our War Against Rape*. New York, Williams Morrow and Company, Inc. 1993. p. 228-29. Hereafter referred to as Fairstein, *Sexual Violence*.

[15] *Ibid.,* p. 58.

[16] *NCVS*, p. 22, 102.

[17] Smith, M. Dwayne and Ellen S. Kuchta. Trends in Violent Crime Against Women, 1973-89. *Social Science Quarterly,* Vol. 75, March 1993. p. 29.

[18] *NCVS*, p. 22; U.S. Department of justice. Bureau of Justice Statistics. *Criminal Victimization in the United States, 1973-90 Trends*. Washington, December 1992. p. 10, 19. Hereafter referred to as *NCVS Trends*.

100,000 inhabitants almost doubled from 1973 (24.5) to 1992 (42.8).[19] The variation in the trends for rape statistics between these two data sources, *NCVS* and *UCR*, may be explained in part by the growing willingness of women to report rape.

A third source for rape statistics is *Rape in America*, a 1992 report prepared by the National Victim Center, in conjunction with a research center at the Medical University of Self The Carolina. This report defines the rape as "any event that occurred without the women's consent, involved the use of force or threat of force, and involved sexual penetration of the victim's vagina, mouth or rectum."[20] The findings of *Rape in America* are based upon a national, longitudinal study of 4,008 women aged 18 years or older. Estimates are provided only for actual rapes, occurring over one year beginning in late 1989.[21]

Rape in America's estimate of 683,000 women raped in 1990 is considerably higher than the number reported in the *UCR* or that estimated by the *NCVS*. Further, the study found that one out of eight or 12.1 million at adult women in the United States, had experienced forcible rape during her lifetime. *Rape in America* cautions that the 683,000 estimate does not include female victims under age 18, nor male victims of rape.[22]

Domestic Assault

Though term "domestic violence" is generally understood to apply to any act of assault committed by a person who either shares a living arrangement with or is involved in an intimate relationship with the victim of the assault. Although there are no official statistics on domestic assault, data provided by the UCR and NCVS may be used in concert to suggest the extent of this problem. Though the *NCVS* does not provide information about murder victims, *UCR* data indicate that police believed that 29 percent of all female murder victims in 1992 were killed by husband or boyfriend, while four percent of all male murder victims were killed by wives or girlfriends.[23] Unlike the *UCR*, the *NCVS* provides more extensive information about the nature of violent crimes committed by intimates on female victims. For example, *NCVS* reports that, between 1979 in 1987, women were three times as likely as men to be victims of violent intimates.[24] Conversely, researchers Murray A. Strauss and Richard J. Gillis found that, between 1975 and 1985,

---

[19] *UCR*, p. 58.

[20] *Rape in America*, p. i.

[21] *Ibid.*, pp. 1-2.

[22] *Rape in America*, pp. 2-3.

[23] *UCR*, p. 17.

[24] *Female Victims of Violent Crime* pp. 1-2.

the rate of violence by men against women decreased, while that by women against men increased.[25]

Domestic violence occurs in one out of every seven couples each year, according to another study, and two-thirds of American couples have been violent at least once during their relationship.[26] The American Medical Association (AMA) estimates that 25 percent of women in United States will be abused by a current or former partner sometime during their lives.[27] The AMA also has called domestic violence a public health problem that has reached "epidemic proportions."[28]

In addition, Senate Judiciary Committee has received testimony from various experts on the extent of the problem of domestic assault: minimum estimates suggest that more than two million women are assaulted yearly by their male partner.[29] According to the most recent survey, completed in 1985, one out of eight husbands committed an act of violence against his spouse. This same survey disclosed that of the 12 percent of the women who were assaulted, more than three out of every 100 women suffered severe injuries.[30]

Sexual Assault on College Campuses

Sexual assaults against women on college campuses are reported to be widespread, with estimates of the number of women raped or sexually assaulted during their college years ranging from one in seven to want in twenty-five.[31] According to a fact sheet prepared by the Senate Judiciary

---

[25] Brott, Armin A. When Women Abuse Men. *Washington Post*. December 28, 1993. p. C5.

[26] Murray A. Straus, as quoted in Facing Battles At Home, *Los Angeles Times*, October 13, 1993, p. B-10, 11.

[27] Hospitals Cope With America's New 'Family Value.' *Hospitals*, v. 66, November 5, 1992. p. 24.

[28] Jecker, Nancy S. Privacy Beliefs and the Violent Family. Journal of the American Medical Association, V. 269, No. 6. February 10, 1993, p. 776.

[29] *Women and Violence,* p. 117. In her testimony Dr. Angela Browne, a Professor of Psychiatry at the University of Massachusetts, suggested that a more accurate nationwide estimate would be 4 million women assaulted yearly by male partners.

[30] *Ibid.* p. 116. In her testimony before the As Senate Judiciary Committee, Dr. Angela Brown noted that the figures she cited were under-estimates. She emphasized that such surveys did not reach women without telephones, non-English-speaking populations, the homeless, those institutionalized, and those unwilling to report acts of violence sustained or perpetrated.
Another study, prepared by the majority staff report of the Senate Judiciary Committee, estimated that nationwide, 1,370, 000 cases of domestic crimes were reported to authorities in 1991. The 17 States that collected such data reported a total of 589,228 cases of domestic violence during the same year. U.S. Congress. Senate. Committee on Judiciary. *Violence Against Women: A Week in the Life of America.* Prepared by the Majority Staff of the Senate Judiciary Committee. Washington, D.C. October 1992. p. 53.

[31] Mathers, Anne. The Campus Crime Wave. *New York times Magazine,* March 7, 1993. p. 38.

Committee, 57 percent of college rape victims are victims of date rape. The Committee reports that the assault rate against women aged 20-24 has increased by 48 percent since 1974, while that for men of the same age group has decreased by 12 percent.[32]

Violence in the Workplace

Statistics relating to safety on the job are further illustrative of the degree to which women are victims of violence. A recent study by the Bureau of Labor Statistics shows that while women are victims in only 7 percent of workplace fatalities, 40 percent of these fatalities are murders.[33]

Characteristics of the Offense of Rape

Selected data are available for rape cases concerning the relationship between the victim and the offender, and in the characteristics of the victim, such as their race/ethnicity, age, marital status, location of residence, and income.

Victim-Offender Relationship

One of the most important aspects of the victim-offender relationship in violent crimes against women is the frequency by which women are attacked by intimates. For example, contrary to the accepted stereotypes that women are most in danger of rape by strangers, a national study found that only 22 percent of all cases fit this category. For the 78 percent who knew their assailant, 9 percent were raped by husbands/ex-husbands, 11 percent by fathers/stepfathers, 10 percent are boyfriends/ex-boyfriends, 16 percent by other relatives, 29 percent by non-relatives such as friends or neighbors, and three percent were not sure or refused to respond.[34]

Though data on the extent of stalking against women are minimal, one expert estimates that up to 90 percent of all women killed by husbands or boyfriends were stalked prior to the crime.[35] According to *UCR* statistics for 1992, 4,936 women were victims of murder, of which 913 were murdered by their husbands and 519 were murdered by boyfriends.[36]

---

[32] U. S. Congress. Senate. Committee on the Judiciary. *Women and Violence.* Hearings, 101st Cong., 2d Sess, Aug. 29, 1990. Washington, U.S. Govt. Print. Off., 1991. p. 78.

[33] U.S. Department of Labor. Bureau of Labor Statistics. *First National Census of Fatal Occupational Injuries Reported by BLS.* USDL-93-406. October 1, 1993. p. 1.

[34] *Rape in America*, p. 4.

[35] Beck, Melinda, *et al.* Murderous Obsession. *Newsweek,* vol. 120, July 13, 1992. p. 61.

[36] *UCR,* pp. 16, 19.

Demographics of Rape Victims

The Bureau of Justice Statistics studied completed and attempted rape of a female victims age 12 and over for the years 1973 through 1987. Using data for the average annual rate of rape per 1,000 women, surveyor's estimated that women in the following categories were the most likely to be raped: (1) those in their late teen years and early twenties, (3) those who were separated or divorced, (4) those living in the central city, and (5) those who are unemployed or have a low family income.[37]

THE RESPONSE OF THE CRIMINAL JUSTICE SYSTEM

The disposition of complaints by female victims of violence within the criminal justice system may vary according to the nature of the crime, the type of complaint, and responses of criminal justice officials. First, the victim must determine whether or not to report the crime. Law enforcement officials on the scene decide if the crime warrants arresting the offender. Judges, prosecutors, and defense attorneys must agree upon the charge and the disposition of the case.

Reporting the Crime

Data suggest that crimes of violence against women are underreported, though the extent of this problem is debated. For example, the *NCVS* study for 1991 states that 59 percent of rapes are reported to the police, while *Rape in America* found that only 16 percent of all rape victims report the offense to the police.[38] Linda Fairstein, an Assistant District Attorney in New York County and the Director of the Sex rimes Prosecution Unit, states that sexual

---

[37] The demographic data for rape victims indicate that: (1) Regarding race, black women (2.7) were almost twice as likely to be raped than white women (1.5). Regarding ethnicity, Hispanic women (1.5) and non-Hispanic women (1.6) had similar rates. (2) Women between the ages of 16 through 19 (4.8) and those between the ages of 20 through 24 (4.1) were the categories most likely to be raped; those younger, aged 12 through 15, and those older were less likely to be raped. (3) Women who were separate or divorced (4.3) and women who have never married (3.5) were almost 6 to 8 times more likely to be raped than married women (.5) and widows (.4). (4) Women who live in the central city (2.5) were approximately twice as likely to be raped than those living in suburbs (1.4) and in non-metropolitan areas (1.1). (5) Approximately half of all women who have been raped are in low family income categories. Women who are unemployed (6.2) are over three times more likely to be raped than those who are employed (1.7). *Female Victims of Violent Crime*, p. 8.

[38] *NCVS*, p. 8; *Rape in America* p. 6.

assault crimes remain the most under-reported cases within the criminal justice system."[39] In addition, a recent study noted that approximately one in four battered women are willing to report their victimization to health professionals on the scene.[40]

According to an *NCVS* study of all female victims of violent crimes who reported the crime to the police from 1973 through 1987, about half stated that they reported the crime to keep it from happening again. Other reasons included a desire to punish the offender, to obtain help after the incident, and to fulfill the victim's duty.[41] Among those victims participating in the study who did not report these crimes to the police, the most common reason given was the respondents' decision that this was a private or personal matter or that she took care of it herself. Other reasons included a fear of reprisal from the offender, his family, or his friends; a belief that the police would not take the report seriously; or a concern that the police would be inefficient, ineffective or insensitive.[42]

Another study, *Rape in America* found that half of all rape victims surveyed would be significantly more willing to report the crime to the police if the news media were unable to obtain and disclose their names and addresses legally.[43] Other reasons provided by criminal justice professionals for the low reportage rate for rape include "ineffective legislation which narrowly defines that permit examination of the character of the victim."[44]

Dispositions

A report by the majority staff of the Senate Judiciary Committee recently criticized the criminal justice system's response to rape, arguing that "over half of all rape prosecutions are either dismissed before trial or result in an acquittal."[45] This figure is based upon *UCR* arrest and offense data for rapes in 1990, from which the report determined that 38 percent of reported

---

[39] Fairstein reports that the majority of criminal justice professionals estimate that less than half of all sex offenses are actually reported. Fairstein, *Sexual Violence*, p. 270.

[40] Glazer, Sarah. Violence Against women. *CQ Researcher*, Vol. 3, February 26, 1993, p. 173. Hereafter referred to as *CQ Researcher*.

[41] *Female Victims of Violent Crime*, p. 3.

[42] *Ibid.*

[43] *Rape in America*

[44] Criminal Justice Politics and Women: The Aftermath of Legally Mandated Change. *Women and Politics*, v. 4, Fall 1984. p. 47.

[45] U.S. Congress. Senate. Committee on the Judiciary. *The Response to Rape: Detours on the Road to Equal Justice.* Report Prepared by the Majority Staff. May 1993. p. 2. Hereafter referred to as *Response to Rape.*

rapes result in an arrest. However, the *UCR* for that year concluded that 52.8 percent of all known offenses for forcible rape were resolved through arrest or by exceptional means.[46]

Also, the majority staff studied 1990 rape data for selected States, from which it determined the following: (1) approximately one out of every 10 rapes reported to the police results in a sentence to prison, (2) only one in every 100 rapes, both reported and unreported, results in a prison sentence greater than one year, (3) approximately one out of every four convicted rapists does not receive a prison sentence, but is placed on probation, and (4) about half of all convicted rapist are incarcerated for less than one year.[47]

Though data for the arrest of those charged with battery of women are unavailable, recent studies suggest that arrest is counterproductive. Criminologist Lawrence W. Sherman found that arresting offenders reduces the number of beating within the immediate 24 hours after the assault, but that such beatings were likely to increase in the long run.[48]

POLICY ISSUES

Federal policy makers have considered legislation in five major areas related to the problem of violence against women: public safety for women; domestic violence; civil rights protection; sexual assault on campuses; and gender bias in the courts.[49]

---

[46] *Ibid.,* p. 65; *UCR*, p. 206-07. The *UCR* defines crimes cleared by exceptional means as follows:

Law enforcement agencies may clear a crime by exceptional means when some element beyond law enforcement control precludes the placing of formal charges against the offender. Examples of circumstances allowing such clearances are the death of the offender (suicide, justifiably killed by police or private citizen, etc.); the victim's refusal to cooperate with prosecution after the offender has been identified; or the denial of extradition because the offender committee another crime and is being prosecuted in a different jurisdiction. IN all exceptional clearance cases, law enforcement must have identified the offender, have enough evidence to support arrest, and know the offender's location.

[47] *Response to Rape*, p. 11.

[48] *CQ Researcher*, p. 174.

[49] The question of gender bias in the courts to relevant because studies have shown that cultural biases regarding women may affect women negatively in their use of the judicial system as claimants in action involving violence.

Public Safety for Women

The same range of solutions that apply to crime control generally also apply to gender-related crimes, and they tend to produce two kinds of recommendations. Some advocates propose tougher prison sentences with the goal of removing wrongdoers from the streets for longer periods of time and, furthermore, of demonstrating that these crimes will be severely punished. Stronger Federal laws, although applying to only a limited number of situations where Federal jurisdiction is primary, also tend to set a standard for those State and local jurisdictions with weaker statutes and to provide a model for reform. Other advocates of change believe that, while legal reforms are needed, they should be augmented by programs to activate community resources,[50] involving the public, law enforcement, and the courts as a means of changing attitudes concerning the problem of public safety for women.[51] To achieve this end, they propose using Federal assistance to fund research and model programs and to test creative, new approaches.

Domestic Violence

Although domestic violence[52] legislation is generally a State and local matter, rather than the responsibility of the congress, there are specific areas in which the Federal government can play a role. Suggested approaches include strengthening protections under interstate statues by expanding the coverage of protective orders so that directives issued in one State are recognized in every other State, enacting legislation to make crossing State lines for the purpose of stalking a Federal offense, making changes in postal service regulations to prevent disclosure of an address to an abusive spouse, and effecting changes in laws relating to immigrant status to assist bettered alien spouses so that they do not have to shield their abuser in order to gain residence.

---

[50] Examples of community resources that might be activated in an education and out-reach campaign include the schools, local

[51] As some have noted, public attitudes about the nature of violence against women are often harder to change than laws. See, Fairstein, Linda. *Sexual Violence: Our War Against Rape.* New York: William Morrow and Co., 1993, p. 17.

[52] The term "domestic violence" is generally understood to apply to any act of assault committed by a person who either shares a living arrangement with or is involved in an intimate relationship with the victim of the assault.

Traditionally, Federal grants have been used to expand State and local programs, especially with regard to improvements in law enforcement efforts, expansion of battered women's shelters, and refinement of judicial procedures.

Although most States have enacted some form of domestic violence legislation,[53] and public recognition of it as a problem has begun, basic attitudes are slow to change. Moreover, approaches that seem effective among some socioeconomic groups tend to fail with others. One example is the debate over treatment of batterers. While early research seemed to indicate that mandatory arrest policies, combined with a few hours behind bars, reduced further battering incidents, additional study showed that it was most effective with those who were not career criminal sand who were employed.[54]

Civil Rights Protection

With the possible exception of the suffrage movement early in this century, discrimination against women was not legislatively recognized as a civil rights issue until the early 1960s. The Civil Rights Act of 1964, narrowly drawn with regard to women, recognizes only gender-based discrimination in the workplace, while the broader problem of attacks on persons, whatever the setting or circumstance, because of their race, religion, or national origin has been a violation of civil rights laws since 1871.[55] Recent legislation has continued this exception. For example, the Hate Crime Statistics Act[56] requires the Justice Department to collect data on crimes motivated by religion, race, sexual orientation, or ethnicity, but not on crimes motivated by gender.

Supporters of federalizing such crimes cite the inadequacies of State remedies. A number of studies conclude that crimes disproportionately affecting women are often treated less seriously in State courts than comparable crimes against men.[57] Proponents also note that State tort laws are inadequate to address crimes motivated by gender, since they typically

---

[53] Glazer, Sarah. *Violence Against Women. CQ Researcher,* p. 178.

[54] Hart, Barbara J. State Codes on Domestic Violence: Analysis, Commentary and Recommendations. *Juvenile and Family Court Journal,* v. 43, no. 4, 1992. p. 70.

[55] Civil Rights Act of 1871 (42 U.S.C. Section 2000(h)).

[56] P.L. 101-275, the Hate Crime Statistics Act, enacted April 23, 1990.

[57] Sind-Flor, Victoria. The Talk of the 9th: Gender Bias. *National Law Journal.* August 17, 1992. p. 3, 43. According to Sind-Flor. Studies of more than 30 State court systems and one Federal circuit tend to verify this conclusion.

focus on physical injuries, such as assault and battery, not on the deprivation of an individual's civil rights. Federal judges and others are concerned that the proposal could overwhelm the Federal courts and think that such cases are better handled at the State level.[58]

Sexual Assault on College Campuses

Under legislation enacted in the 102d Congress, schools are required to collect statistics on campus crime, including sex crimes, and to develop, publish, and distribute information regarding campus security policies and law enforcement.[59] Some have suggested building on P.L. 102-325 by continuing the funding necessary to carry out the provisions relating to campus crimes against women. Other proposals would go a step further and authorize a Department of Justice study of the problem of campus sexual crimes and of the effectiveness of efforts to address the problem.

These two approaches seem complementary. Authorizing a specific dollar amount to be spent on campus sexual assault prevention and for collecting data on crimes against women would tend to highlight prevention and documentation of campus sex crimes. At present, sex offenses are one of a number of crimes designated by P.L. 102-325 for policy and program definition and tabulation, and the funding is not specifically allocated. The study proposed would ensure that the data collected by individual institutions would be aggregated and then applied to a specific use nationally, possibly assisting colleges to refine their security policies to achieve greater effectiveness.

Gender Bias in the Courts

Since the State of New Jersey published the first survey of gender bias in its courts in 1983, the incidence of gender bias in the judicial system has been documented by at least 30 other States, as well as by the U.S. Ninth

---

[58] Prior to passage in the Senate Judiciary Committee, a new Title VI was added to S. 2754 to include language specifying that disputes such as divorce proceedings or property settlements would not be eligible for hearing in Federal courts.

[59] Although P.L. 102-325 requires all colleges and universities receiving Federal funds to publish annually their security and crime-reporting policies, and to make public the number of on-campus incidents of sexual assault and other designated crimes, the law does not require that the campus-crime data be analyzed.

Judicial Circuit.[60] These studies have found that bias pervades almost every aspect of the court process and includes attitudes concerning women as litigants, attorneys, and employees.

In assisting States to make changes in judicial practices system-wide some have proposed that the Federal Government fund programs of education and training for judges and court personnel concerning evidence of existing social and economic bias against women. Over the past 30 years, the law has been evolving in the area of women's rights, creating more women litigants who are presenting new kinds of claims on the legal system. More women also are now lawyers and employees of the court system with problems related to such issues as professional acceptance, harassment, and low pay scales. One study concluded that the courts have a "special obligation to reject – not reflect – societies irrational prejudices."[61] In addition, in response to complaints of abuse of the client-attorney relationship, proposals have been suggested relating to ethics reform to forbid certain kinds of arguably egregious behavior against women clients.

LEGISLATION

Recent Initiatives

Legislation proposing a Federal response to the problem of violence against women was first introduced in 1990. Over the next several y ears, a number of hearings were held, primarily in the Senate, with the Senate Judiciary Committee ordering bills reported in the 101st, 102d, and 103d Congresses.[62]

A variety of measures to address the problem of violence against women was introduced in the 103d Congress. Among those bills pursuing a criminal justice approach, S. 6 (Dole), S. 11 (Biden), and H.R. 688 (Molinari) are designed to prevent and punish sexual violence and domestic violence, and provide assistance and protection to victims. In addition, several omnibus crime bills, including H.R. 2847 (Sensenbrenner), H.R. 2872 (McCollum), and S.8 (Hatch), contain provisions related to violence against women. The

---

[60] See, Five Year Report of the New York Judicial Committee on Women in the courts. *Fordham Urban Law Journal*, V. 19, Winter 1992 p. 313-390; The Talk of the Ninth: Circuit Faces the Future. *National Law Journal*, August 17, 1992. p. 3, 43; Reports Track Discrimination: Fourteen Volumes Chronicle How Women Are treated in Court, *National Law Journal,* November 20, 1990. p. 1, 24, 25.

[61] Five Year Report of the New York Judicial Committee on Women in the Courts. P. 316.

[62] For example, see S. 2754 (Biden), S. 15 (Biden, and S. 11 (Biden), respectively.

House and Senate have passed H.R. 1133(Schroeder) and S. 1607 (Biden), repetitively. Both bills contain provisions pertaining to violence against women. The text of S. 1607 was inserted by the Senate into H.R. 3355, and passed as amended.

In a related area, the 103d Congress is considering several measures to address the problem of stalking. For example, H.R. 740 (Royce), H.R. 1133 (Schroeder), H.R. 1461 (Mfume), and S. 470 (Boxer) would provide criminal penalties for stalking; and H.R. 840 (Kennedy) would establish a national program to reduce its incidence.

Since 1990, 48 States and the District of Columbia have enacted anti-staling legislation, but many of these statutes have been too broadly or too narrowly drawn to provide effective redress. In 1992 Congress established task force in the National Institute of Justice (NIJ) to develop model anti-stalking legislation that would be both constitutional and enforceable. On October 4, 1993, NIJ completed the study and issued several recommendations, including the use of a series of graduated penalties and the revision of the State bail, probation, and parole procedures to protect victims.[63]

Violence Against Women Provisions in H.R. 3355/S. 1607 and H.R. 1133

On November 19, 1993, the Senate passed H.R. 3355, amended, containing provisions related to violence against women (Titles 32-37). The House passed H.R. 1133 on November 20, 1993. A conference on the differences between the two measures is scheduled early in the second session of the 103d Congress.

Because rape, sexual assault, domestic violence, and other such crimes are primarily a State and local responsibility, Federal jurisdiction is limited to specific areas within its control, including interstate commerce, Federal prisons, and special maritime and territorial jurisdictions, such as military and naval enclaves, Indian reservations, and national parks. As a result, the legislation, approved in November 1993 by each chamber, would effect changes through amendments of the *U.S.Code* to improve Federal practices and strengthen penalties through amendments to Federal law in areas where

---

[63] Statement of Senator William S. Cohen. Congressional Record. Daily edition. Vol. 139, October 4, 1993. p. S12901; A Stalking Statute. *Washington Post*. September 17, 1993. p. A20.

interstate jurisdiction is required and through grants to States and localities to fund reforms.

The proposed legislation consists of a multi-part program of reforms designed to prevent and punish rape, domestic violence, sexual assault, and other violent crimes against women. It would increase penalties for sex crimes, provide restitution for victims, encourage States to increase arrest and prosecution rates, and fund programs for State and Federal judges and other court personnel to overcome attitudinal barriers related to women victims and gender-based crimes. The House bill, H.R. 1133, is similar to the Senate measure, H.R. 3355/S. 1607, in many of its provisions, but places less emphasis on amending the *U.S. Code* to create harsher penalties and more on education and prevention programs to effect social and cultural change as a method of reducing sexual assaults.

Public Safety for Women

Under the Senate bill, Federal penalties for rape, aggravated rape, and repeated sex offenses would be doubled, new penalties would be created for recidivists, and restitution mandated for victims of sex crimes. Proposals to encourage women to prosecute their attackers include limitation of the circumstances under which evidence of the past sexual behavior may be introduced, extension of rape shield law protection to criminal and civil cases, and barring the use of clothing to claim that the victim incited or invited a sexual assault. The Senate bill would require pre-trial detention for felony offenses under Federal sexual and child abuse statutes, and would require the Government to pay for human immunodeficiency virus tests and for any related counseling session. Both the Senate and House proposals would require States to pay for all forensic rape examinations and would provide for mandatory restitution to a victim of a sex crime.

Grant programs under both House and Senate bills would highlight the escalating problem of public safety for women by spurring State and local action toward the revision of laws and procedures relating to sex crimes. The House bill concentrates primarily on programs to combat violent crime against women through training of law enforcement personnel and prosecutors, strengthening of victim service programs, and improvement of State and local education and prevention programs to help change public attitudes regarding sexual assault. The Senate bill also would provide for capital improvements to prevent crime on public transportation and in national and public parks.

Domestic Violence

Provisions of both bills would create the first Federal laws on spouse abuse, remedying a gap in State law relating to protective orders, so that orders issued in one State would have the same effect in all other States, and Federal penalties, in addition to any State penalties, would be levied for crossing State lines to injure, harass, or intimidate a spouse or intimate partner. The Senate bill would triple funding to shelter victims of abuse and require States to explore new legal protections for victims. Under the House bill, an alleged victim would be given an opportunity to be heard regarding the danger posed by the release of the defendant and restitution to the victim would be required, in addition to any fine or prison term imposed.

To maintain the confidentiality of addresses of victims of domestic violence, the Senate bill would prohibit disclosure under Postal Service regulations, following presentation of a court order or an affidavit. The Attorney General would be asked to study methods used by abusive spouses to obtain such information as well as ways in which victims might keep such information confidential. The House bill provides only for a study of the confidentiality issue.

Under an amendment to the Immigration and Nationality Act[64] proposed in the House bill, battered or divorced immigrant spouses and their children would be permitted the right to self-petition for immigrant status, removing the requirement for a petition initiated by a citizen spouse or former spouse.

A number of grant programs also are proposed. Both bills would encourage arrests in domestic violence cases through the Department of Justice grants to State and local governments and Indian tribes. These grants would be used for training of police department, tracking and centralization of cases, legal advocacy programs for victims, and improvement of judicial handling. Other grants under the Senate and House bills would strengthen State and local efforts to prevent and punish domestic violence through training , model programs, and outreach efforts. Funding of battered women's shelters would be increased substantially over the present authorization of $25 million per year, and grants through the Department of Education would be made available for educating young people about domestic violence and violence among intimate partners.

The Senate proposal also would require the Attorney General to report to Congress regarding the status of battered women's syndrome as a medical and psychological condition and on the effect of admitting such evidence on criminal trials. It would also require the Judicial Conference to report to

---

[64] 8 U.S.C. 1154.

Congress on amending Federal Rules of Evidence to allow testimony regarding an alleged rapist's prior sex crimes in rape trials and to evaluate the need for a code of ethics for cases involving sexual misconduct by lawyers in the Federal system.

Civil Rights
The Senate bill would label sex crimes as "bias" or "hate" crimes that deprive victims of their civil rights, extend Federal civil rights protections to all gender-motivated crimes, and allow victims of crimes "motivated by gender" to bring civil rights suits against their assailants. Crimes covered would include felony rape, sexual assault, and kidnapping. Victims would be able to recover compensatory and punitive damages, injunctive and declaratory relief, or any combination of these awards. The proposal would preclude involvement of the Federal court in child custody, child support, alimony, divorce proceedings, or domestic relations disputes where violence is claimed. Sponsors note that it would not create a general Federal law for all assaults or rapes against women.

A similar proposal in the House bill as introduced was omitted by the Judiciary Subcommittee on Crime and Criminal Justice, as a subject area beyond its jurisdiction.

Sexual Assault on College Campuses
The Senate bill would authorize $20 million in Federal grant money for FY1994, with additional sums in subsequent years, to carry out the provisions of the 1992 Higher Education Act (P.L. 102-325) specifically relating to campus crimes against women. The House bill would expand the reach of P.L. 102-325 to authorize a Department of Justice baseline study to examine the scope of the problem of campus sexual assaults and the effectiveness of institutional and legal policies in addressing such crimes and protecting victims. An appropriation of $200,000 would be authorized for this purpose.

Gender Bias in the Courts
Both bills would authorize grants through the Department of Justice for model programs to be used for education and training for State judges and court personnel to decrease stereotyping of women victims and increase sensitivity about domestic violence, rape, sexual assault, and gender bias. Program materials would include laws governing rape, sexual assault, domestic violence, and other crimes of violence motivated by the victim's gender. Also included would be the nature and incidence of rape; the

physical, psychological, and economic impact of rape and domestic violence on the victim; the application of rape shield laws; the use of testimony on the rape trauma syndrome; and the legitimate reasons why women victims of crimes do not report those crimes. Also authorized would be studies of gender bias in Federal circuit courts, and the Federal Judicial Center would be directed to include information on gender bias in its educational program, including training of Federal judges and court personnel.

Under the Senate proposal, the Judicial Conference would be asked to consider whether Federal rules of ethics ought to be created for lawyers in Federal cases involving sexual misconduct, such as distressing or harassing behavior or activities designed solely to increase the costs of litigation.

Alternative Viewpoints

Critics of recent legislative efforts to address the problem of violence against women raise a variety of concerns First, they argue that this initiative singles out women for increased protections, but ignores violence perpetrated against men, especially offenses involving female attacks on men and sexual assault on male prisoners by other inmates. Second, recent legislative initiatives have penalized offenses against women as hate crimes, although existing Federal laws do not include gender as a hate crime category. Finally, critics argue that adding offenses against women to a growing list of Federal crimes is a waste of resources and a needless intrusion upon the police power of the States.

Several recent studies have shown that the problem of women's violence against men is more extensive than it has been believed. For example, researchers Murray Straus, Richard Gelles, and others conducted major surveys of family violence in 1975 and in 1985. They found that men are equally likely to be victims of domestic violence as women and that during this decade the rate of male-on-female violence declined while that for female-on-male violence increased.[65] In addition, Suzanne Steinmetz, director of the Family Research Institute at Indiana University-Purdue University, explains that men are taught to limit their inclination to respond

---

[65] Brott, Armin A. When Women Abuse Men. *Washington Post*. December 28, 1993. p. C5. Brott notes that the relative size of men and women enables men to inflict greater harm with their fists, but adds that this advantage is often neutralized by women's use of weapons. A study of 6,200 cases of domestic assault found that 86 percent of female on male violence involved weapons; conversely, weapons were used in 25 percent of male on female violence.

physically to their partner's verbal abuse or violence.[66] Most importantly, there is extensive anecdotal support that men greatly under-report violence perpetrated upon them by their spouses, because they fear ridicule and are inclined to believe they will appear weak if they do so.

Another criticism of the focus on violence against women concerns the corresponding lack of protection of male prisoners from sexual assault by other inmates. Stephen Donaldson, president of Stop Prisoner Rape, reports that every year over 290,000 males are sexually assaulted while incarcerated, a number one and a half to two times greater than the number of rapes of women a year reported by the Bureau of Justice Statistics.[67] He maintains:

> While prison officials private concede the existence of this widespread pattern of abuse, prisoner victims are ignored in national rape statistics and estimates, and little has been done to stop the attacks. . . . While some prison system professionals want to address the problem, most prefer to ignore it; no doubt many see it as a public relations embarrassment rather than the life-and-death issue it has become in the age of AIDS.[68]

Second, when Congress enacted the Hate Crime Statistics Act of 1990 (P.L. 101-275), it did not include one's sex as a category of which the Department of Justice must collect statistics in its annual report of hate crime nationwide. Though some legislators urged that gender be included and asserted that current data collection for such crimes against women as rape and domestic violence were deficient, Congress chose not to do so.[69] Therefore, recent legislative initiatives penalizing offenses against women as hate crimes do not necessarily resolve the debate about whether or not such offenses should be enumerated among hate crimes.

Another major concern of critics involves the growing number of offenses that have been penalized at the Federal level. They maintain that the establishment of Federal statutes for violence against women will ring "a host of domestic issues into federal courts."[70] Critics complain that the federalization of such crimes not only intrudes upon the traditional jurisdiction of States in this area, it also forces Federal courts "to deal with

---

[66] *Ibid.*

[67] Donaldson, Stephen. The Rape Crisis Behind Bars. *Washington Post*, December 29, 1993. p. A11.

[68] *Ibid.*

[69] Fernandez, Joseph M. Bringing Hate Crime Into Focus -- the Hate Crime Statistics Act of 1990, Pub. L. No. 101-275. *Harvard Civil Rights-Civil Liberties law Review.* Vol. 26, Winter 1991, p. 275.

[70] Wagar, Linda. Federal Overkill. *State Government News.* April 1992. p. 12.

so many Federal crimes it's hurting their traditional, civil role: protecting people's constitutional and civil rights."[71]

---

[71] Bendavid, Naftali. How Much More Can Courts, Prisons Take? *Legal Times.* Vol. 16, June 7, 1993. pp. 1, 22.

Chapter 2

VIOLENCE AGAINST WOMEN ACT: REAUTHORIZATION, FEDERAL FUNDING AND RECENT DEVELOPMENTS

Alison Siskin

SUMMARY

On October 26, 2000, the President signed a five-year reauthorization of appropriations for the Violence Against Women Act, expired at the end of FY2000, together with an expansion of its programs (VAWA, title IV of the Violent Crime Control and Law Enforcement Act, P.L. 103-322). On October 11, 2000, the Senate approved the conference report, H.Report. 106-939, for the Sexual Trafficking Victims Protection Act (H.R. 3244/Smith, Christopher). Approved by the House on October 6, 2000, the measure contains language to reauthorize the Violence Against Women Act (VAWA), as amended. The conference report notes that the bill reauthorizes through FY2005 the leading VAWA programs, and makes "targeted improvements," such as authorizing grants for legal assistance for victims of domestic violence, stalking, and sexual assault; providing funding for transitional housing assistance, improving full faith and credit enforcement and computerized tracking of protection orders, strengthening and refining the protections for battered immigrant women, and expanding existing grant programs to cover violence that arises in dating relationship.

VAWA was enacted in 1994 and became law after a long campaign to impose national social and criminal sanctions against those who commit violent acts against women, acts including sexual assault, domestic violence, and stalking. Between FY1995 and FY2000, Congress steadily increased funding for most of Title IV's grant programs. In FY2000 the amount appropriated for programs under VAWA was $435. 75 million For FY2001, Congress appropriated $407.8 million for VAWA programs. A right delineated under Title IV that allowed individuals to sue in federal court for gender-motivated crimes was declared unconstitutional by the Supreme Court on May 15, 2000. Untouched by the Court ruling were all other provisions of VAWA -- a number of grant programs to the states, together with mandatory studies intended to document the extent of the problem of violence against women and to point toward possible solutions.

VIOLENCE AGAINST WOMEN: BACKGROUND AND STATISTICS

Statistics on crimes of violence against women depict a personal safety problem that some believe may seriously limit the ability of threatened women to function fully in American society. Such crimes often have devastating consequences for these women personally, as well as for their families and for society as a whole. Since FY1995, a major source of funding for programs to reduce rape, stalking, and domestic violence has been the Violence Against Women Act (P.S. 103-322, Title IV). The Departments of Justice (DOJ) and Health and Human Services (HHS) administer a number of grants under VAWA, and their reports on addressing or preventing gender-related crimes are submitted annually to Congress. Prior to the existence of these reports, empirical data were limited on the interrelationships between certain types of violence against women, such as childhood victimization and subsequent adult victimization. The data being collected under VAWA are intended to help define the extent of the problem of violence against women and point toward possible solutions. Based on this survey data, the 1998 collaborative study on violence jointly funded by DOJ and HHS[1] report that:

---

[1] U.S. Department of Justice, National Institute of Justice, Office of Justice Programs, and Department of Health and Human Services, Centers for Disease Control and Prevention, *Prevalence, Incidence, and Consequences of Violence Against Women: Findings from the National Violence Against Women Survey* (Washington: November 1998), p. 2. The principal source for crime data has long been the FBI's Uniform Crime Reporting (UCR)

- Using a definition of rape that includes forced vaginal, oral, and anal intercourse, nearly 18% of women in the United States said they have been raped (14.8%) or the victim of an attempted rape (2.8%) in their lifetime. Based on these survey figures. 17.7 million women are projected to have been raped. More than half of the rape victims said they were under age 17 when first raped. Of the women who reported being raped at some time in their lives, 22% were under 12 years old and 32% were 12 to 17 years old when they were first raped.

- Differences in the prevalence of reported rape and physical assault among women of different racial and ethnic backgrounds are statistically significant: American Indian/Alaska Native women were most likely to report these crimes, Asian/Pacific Islander women were least likely to report them, and Hispanic women were less likely to make such reports than non-Hispanic women.

- Physical assault, ranging from slapping and hitting to gun violence, is widespread: 52% of women said they were physically assaulted as a child by an adult caretaker or as an adult by any type of perpetrator, and 1.9% of women said they were physically assaulted in the previous 12 months. Based on the survey figures, approximately 1.9 million women are projected to be physically assaulted annually in the United States.

- Women report significantly more partner violence than do men: 29% of women, compared with 8% of men, said they were raped or physically assaulted or both in their lifetime by a current or former spouse, cohabiting partner, or date; 1.5% of women and 0.9% of men said they were raped or physically assaulted by such a perpetrator in the previous 12 months. According to survey estimates, approximately 1.5 million women and 834,700 men are projected to be raped or physically assaulted by an intimate partner annually in the United States.[2]

Program, a compilation of monthly law enforcement reports and individual crime incident records voluntarily submitted. Since crimes against women are believed to be underreported in the UCR, data for collaborative DOJ-HHS survey were based on a nationally representative telephone survey of 8,000 women and 8,000 men. The survey was designed to protect confidentiality and minimize the potential for retraumatizing victims. Differences in data collection methods explain the differences between the collaborative survey and the UCR.

[2] For men, the reported under number of rape victims was statistically insignificant.

- Violence against adult women is primarily partner violence: 76% of the women (compared to 18% of men) who were raped or physically assaulted or both since age 18 said the perpetrator was a current or former spouse, a co-habiting partner, or a date.

- Women are significantly more apt to be insured during an assault: 32% of women and 16% of men who reported they were raped since 18 said they were injured during their most recent rape; 39% of the women and 25% of the men who were physically assaulted since age 18 were injured during their most recent physical assault. About one in three women who were injured during a physical assault required medical care.

- Stalking is more prevalent than previously thought: using a definition of stalking that involves repeated visual or physical proximity; non-consensual communication; verbal, written or implied threats; or a combination of these that would cause a victim to feel a high level of fear, 8% of women and 2% of men said they were stalked at some time in their lives. According to survey estimates, approximately one million women and 371,000 men are projected to be stalked annually in the United States.

LEGISLATIVE SUMMARY AND SUPREME COURT RULING

Legislation proposing a federal response to the problem of violence against women was first introduced in 1990, in part due to pressure from organized women's groups. Congressional action to address gender-related violence culminated in the enactment of the Violent Crime Control and Law Enforcement Act of 1994.[3] Under its Title IV, the Violence Against Women Act, known as VAWA, a provision was included that would have permitted private damage suits in federal court by victims of "gender motivated violence." This provision was struck down (5-4) on May 15, 2000, by the Supreme Court in *United States v. Morrison* as unconstitutional under the Commerce Clause and the Fourteenth Amendment. This provision would have permitted private damage suits in federal court by victims of "gender

---

[3] (P.L. 103-322, 108 Stat. 1902, 42 U.S.C. 1370). See: CRS Report 94-910, *Crime Control: Summary of the Violent Crime Control and Law Enforcement Act of 1994*, coordinated by Charles Doyle, p. 32-48.

motivated violence." The Court fund that such violence does not substantially affect interstate commerce. It further noted that the Fourteenth Amendment is directed at state actions, not those of private citizens.

Unaffected by the Court decision were grant programs established under VAWA and created within DOJ and HHS. These programs are administered by the states and funds can be allocated by the states to state agencies, Indian tribal governments, units of local government and private nonprofit groups. They include grants to improve law enforcement and prosecution of violent crimes against women, grants to encourage arrests in domestic violence incidents, moneys for rural domestic violence and child abuse enforcement, rape prevention and education programs, and grants for battered women's shelters, among others. (A national domestic violence hotline is funded to a single contractor directly out of HHS.)[4] Funding was authorized through FY2000 under the Violent Crime Reduction Trust Fund (VCRTF), created under Title XXXI of the Violent Crime Control and Law Enforcement Act of 1994.

The 106th Congress approved the reauthorization of VAWA grant programs, amended, under Division B, the Violence Against Women Act of 2000, in the Sexual Trafficking Victims Protection Act (H.R. 3244/Smith, Christopher). The President signed the bill on October 26, 2000. VAWA 2000 reauthorizes from FY2001-FY2005 the key VAWA programs. Also, the bill authorizes grants for legal assistance for victims of domestic violence, stalking, and sexual assault; provides funding for transitional housing assistance; improves full faith and credit enforcement and computerized tracking of protection orders; strengthens and refines the protections for battered immigrant women; authorizes grants for supervised visitation and safe visitation exchange of children between parents in situations involving domestic violence, child abuse, sexual assault, or stalking; and expands several of they key grant programs to cover violence that arises in dating relationships. As approved, H.R. 3244 superceded two earlier measures to reauthorize VAWA, H.R. 1248/Morella, and S.2787/Biden and Hatch. Hr. R. 1248 was passed by the House, amended, on September 26, 2000, and S. 2787 was reported by the Senate Judiciary Committee on July 12, 2000.

---

[4] The current and past funding levels of these programs are listed in the table at the end of this report.

FUNDING UNDER THE VIOLENCE
AGAINST WOMEN ACT

The FY2000 amount enacted for VAWA programs was $453.25 million, $17.5 million less than the amount enacted for FY1999 and $1.0 million more than the President's Fy2000 request.[5] For FY2001, the President requested $481 million and Congress appropriated $407.8 million for VAWA programs, however, funding for VAWA programs created in the original Act did not truly decrease. Grants to Prevent Sexual Abuse of Runaways and Homeless Youth were reauthorized in the Missing, Exploited, and Runway Children Protection Act (P.L. 106-71), and received appropriations of $15 million for FY2001. In addition, the Center for Disease Control received $176 million for Prevention Grants such as Rape Education and Prevention and Community Domestic Violence Programs, but the appropriations bill failed to specify specific amounts for the different programs. Assuming FY2001 funding levels from the prevention grants remain at FY2000 levels funding for VAWA programs increased by $20 million between FY2000 and FY2001. As the table below shows, not all of the programs enacted under VAWA have been funded continuously; some have received money for a brief period only, while others have never been funded.

---

[5] Consolidated Appropriations Act for FY2000 (P.L. 106-113) signed by President Clinton on Oct. 29, 1999. *See source note at end of table for complete Congressional Record citation.)

Table 1. Violence Against Women Program Funding, FY1995 through FY 2001 (budget authority in millions)

Program	Admin. agency	FY1995 enacted	FY1995 enacted	FY1997 enacted	FY1998 enacted	FY1999 enacted	FY2000 enacted	FY2001 enacted
Law Enforcement and Prosecution Grants (STOP" Grants) (Sec. 40121)	QJP	26.00	130.00	145.00	172.00	206.75	206.75	210.8
Grants to Encourage Arrest Policies (Sec. 40231)	QJP	0	28.00	33.00	59.00	34.00	34.00	34.00
Rural Domestic Violence and Child Abuse Enforcement (Sec. 40295)	QJP	0	7.00	8.00	25.00	25.00	25.00	25.00
Court Appointed Special Advocates for Victims of Child Abuse (Sec. 40156c)	QJP	0	6.00	6.00	7.00	9.00	10.00	11.50
Training for Judicial Personnel and Practitioners for Victims of Child Abuse (Sec. 156b)	QJP	0	0.75	1.00	2.00	2.00	2.00	2.00
Grants for Televised Testimony by Victims of Child Abuse (Sec. 20156c)	QJP	0	0.05	0.55	1.00	1.00	1.00	1.00
National Stalker and Domestic Violence Reduction Grants (Sec. 40603)	QJP	0	1.50	1.75	2.75	0	0	0
Training Programs for Probation and Parole Offices Who Work with Released Sex Offenders (Sec. 40152)	QJP	0	1.00	1.00	2.00	5.00	5.00	5.00

Program	Admin. agency	FY1995 enacted	FY1995 enacted	FY1997 enacted	FY1998 enacted	FY1999 enacted	FY2000 enacted	FY2001 enacted
National Study on Campus Sexual Assault (Sec. 40506)	QJP	0	0	0.20	0	0	0	0
State Databases Studies (Sec. 40292)	QJP	0	0.20	0	0	0	0	0
Federal Victim Counselors (Sec. 40114)	USA	0	0	1.00	1.00	0	0	0
Subtotal: Department of Justice		26.00	174.50	197.50	270.75	282.75	283.75	288.68
Training Judges/Court Personnel (Sec. 40421-22)		0	0	0	0	0	0	0
Subtotal: The Judiciary		0	0	0	0	0	0	0
Equal Justice for Women in Courts/Training Grants (Sec. 40411-14)		0	0	0	0	0	0	0
Subtotal: State Justice Institute		0	0	0	0	0	0	0
National Domestic Violence Hotline (Sec. 40211)	ACF	1.00	0.00	1.20	1.20	1.20	2.00	2.16

Program	Admin. agency	FY1995 enacted	FY1995 enacted	FY1997 enacted	FY1998 enacted	FY1999 enacted	FY2000 enacted	FY2001 enacted
Grants to Reduce Sexual Abuse of Runaway, Homeless, and Street Youth (Sec. 40155)	ACF	0	5.56	8.00	15.00	15.00	15.00	15.00[a]
Grants for Battered Women Shelters (Sec. 40241)	ACF	0	15.00	10.80	76.80	88.80	101.50	116.92
Youth Education and Domestic Violence (Sec. 40251)	ACF	0	0	0	0	0	0	0
National Number and Cost of Injuries Study (Sec. 40293)	CDC	0	0.10	0	0	0	0	0
Rape Prevention and Education Grants (Sec. 40151)	CDC	0	28.54	35.00	45.00	45.00	45.00	[b]
Immunity Programs on Domestic Violence (Sec. 40261)	CDC	0	3.00	6.00	6.00	6.00	6.00	
Total: Department of Health and Human Services		1.00	52.60	61.00	144.00	156.00	169.50	119.08
Safety for Women: Capital Improvements to Prevent Crime in National Parks (Sec. 40132)		0	0	0	0	0	0	0
Safety for Women: Capital Improvements to Prevent Crime in Public Parks (Sec. 40133)		0	0	0	0	0	0	0

Program	Admin. agency	FY1995 enacted	FY1995 enacted	FY1997 enacted	FY1998 enacted	FY1999 enacted	FY2000 enacted	FY2001 enacted
Total: Department of the Interior		0	0	0	0	0	0	0
Safety for Women: Capital Improvements to Prevent Crime in Public Transportation (Sec. 40131)		0	0	0	0	0	0	0
Subtotal: Department of Transportation		0	0	0	0	0	0	0
Grand Total		27.00	227.10	258.50	420.75	438.75	453.25	407.76

Sources: For FY1995-FY2000 funding information, see *Budget of the United States Government: Appendix* for indicated years under named agencies. For FY2001 funding information, see FY2001: Commerce, Justice State Appropriations (P.L. 106-553), and FY2001: Labor, Health and Human Services, and Education Appropriations (P.L. 106-554).

[a] These grants were reauthorized through FY2003 by the Missing, Exploited, and Runway Children Protection Act (P.L. 106-71; S. 249/Hatch), which was signed into law on October 12, 1999. Thus, these monies are not included in the total of VAWA funds for FY2001.

[b] These grants were not specified by name in the appropriations bill. However, in H.R. 4577 the CDC was allocated $175.97 million for prevention grants, which would include these programs. $44 million for rape prevention was mentioned in the House Appropriations committee report, but not included in the bill.

Abbreviations to TABLE.

In DOJ: USA (United States Attorneys), QJP (Office of Justice Programs)

In HHS: ACF (Administration for Children and Families), CDC (Centers for Disease Control and Prevention)

Chapter 3

Sexual Harassment and Violence Against Women: Developments in Federal Law

Charles V. Dale

Summary

Gender-based discrimination, harassment, and violence against women in the workplace and society generally have assumed new legal and political significance as a consequence of recent high profile proceedings involving alleged misdeeds by elected government officials, members of the military, public school teachers and students, and the private corporate sector. This chapter reviews the judicial evolution of sexual harassment law, including a discussion of four recent U.S. Supreme Court rulings that dealt with the issue of same-sex harassment and determined the liability of employers and school districts for harassment by supervisory employees and acts directed against public school students.

During its 1997-98 term, the U.S. Supreme Court decided four cases involving a range of issues from the legality of same-sex harassment to the vicarious liability of employers and a local school district for monetary damages as the result of harassment by supervisors and teachers. In *Oncale v. Sundowner Offshore Services Inc.,* the U.S. Supreme Court resolved a conflict among the federal circuit courts by ruling that sex discrimination consisting of same-sex harassment is actionable under Title VII. *Faragher v. City of Boca Raton* and *Burlington Industries v. Ellerth*, held employers vicariously liable for sexual harassment of an employee by a supervisor with immediate or successively higher authority of that employee. Where the harassment results in a "tangible employment action"—such as demotion or discharge—against the victim, Title VII liability is automatic and no defense is available to the employer. In cases not involving tangible reprisals or loss of job benefits, however, the failure of a complaining employee to take advantage of any anti-harassment policy and procedures made available by the employer may be asserted as an affirmative defense. *Doe v. Lago Vista Independent School District*, by contrast, ruled 5 to 4 that Title IX of the Education Amendments of 1972 imposes no liability on local school districts for teacher harassment of students unless a school official with authority to institute corrective measures has actual knowledge of the alleged misconduct and is deliberately indifferent to it.

INTRODUCTION

Gender-based discrimination, harassment, and violence against women in the home, workplace, and society at large have been the focus of considerable legislative and judicial attention in recent years. Legal doctrines condemning the extortion of sexual favors as a condition of employment or job advancement, and other sexually offensive workplace behaviors resulting in a "hostile environment," continue to evolve from judicial decisions under Title VII of the 1964 Civil Rights Act and other federal equal employment opportunity laws. In 1994, Congress broke new legal ground by creating a civil rights cause of action for victims of "crimes of violence motivated by gender." The new law also made it a federal offense to travel interstate with the intent to "injure, harass, or intimidate" a spouse, causing bodily harm to the spouse by a crime of violence.[1] On May 16, 2000, however, the Supreme Court decided in *U.S. v. Morrison*[2] that Congress had overstepped its constitutional bounds when it passed the VAWA civil remedy provision and invalidated the statute.

Sexual harassment issues have recently assumed new legal and political importance. The military conviction of a drill sergeant at the Army's Aberdeen training facility for rape and sexual harassment of female recruits, and recent allegations by the Army's highest ranking female general that she

---

[1] 18 U.S.C. Sec. 2261(a)(1).

was harassed by a male colleague, have focused the public's attention once more upon sexual harassment in the military. Similarly, proceedings leading to the dismissal of sexual harassment charges against the President by a former Arkansas state employee spawned a host of legal and constitutional issues that may reverberate for years to come. Questions as to the legal responsibility of school districts or other educational authorities for sexual harassment within the schools are highlighted by judicial decisions and numerous alleged incidents of sexual abuse or unwanted displays of affection involving public school students and their teachers.

During its 1997-98 term, the U. S. Supreme Court decided four cases involving a range of issues from the legality of same-sex harassment to the vicarious liability of employers and a local school district for monetary damages as the result of harassment by supervisors and teachers. On March 4th, 1998, the U.S. Supreme Court resolved a conflict among the federal circuit courts by ruling, in *Oncale v. Sundowner Offshore Services Inc.*[3] that sex discrimination consisting of same-sex harassment is actionable under Title VII. *Faragher v. City of Boca Raton*[4] and *Burlington Industries v. Ellerth*[5] dramatically altered the standards that had been applied by federal appeals courts to determine employer Liability in sexual harassment cases. Where harassment by a supervisor results in a "tangible employment action"—such as demotion or discharge—against an employee, Title VII liability is automatic and no defense is available to the employer. In cases not involving tangible reprisals or loss of job benefits, however, the fact that a complaining employee "unreasonably" failed to avail herself of any anti-harassment policy and procedures established by the employer may be asserted as an affirmative defense. *Gebser v. Lago Vista Independent School District*,[6] by contrast, ruled 5 to 4 that Title IX of the Education Amendments of 1972 imposes no liability on local school districts for teacher harassment of students unless a school official with authority to institute corrective measures has actual knowledge of the alleged misconduct and is deliberately indifferent to it. Relying on *Gebser*, the Court in *Davis v. Monroe County Board of Education*[7] recognized that school districts may also be liable for student-on-student harassment, but only where responsible officials "are deliberately indifferent to sexual harassment, of which they have actual knowledge, that is so severe, pervasive, and objectively

---

[2] 120 S. Ct. 1740 (2000).
[3] 523 U.S. 75 (1998)
[4] 524 U.S. 775 (1998)
[5] 524 U.S. 742 (1998)
[6] 524 U.S. 274 (1998)
[7] 526 U.S. 629 (1999)

offensive that it can be said to deprive the victims of access to the educational opportunities or benefits provided by the school."

FEDERAL EQUAL EMPLOYMENT OPPORTUNITY LAW

Title VII of the 1964 Civil Rights Act does not mention sexual harassment but makes it unlawful for employers with 15 or more employees to discriminate against any applicant or employee "because of sex."[8] Federal law on the subject is, therefore, largely a judicial creation, having evolved over nearly a three-decade period from federal court decisions and guidelines of the Equal Employment Opportunity Commission (EEOC) interpreting Title VII's sex discrimination prohibition.[9] Two forms of sexual harassment have been recognized by the courts and EEOC administrative guidelines. The first, or *"quid pro quo"* harassment, occurs when submission to "unwelcome" sexual advances, propositions, or other conduct of a sexual nature is made an express or implied condition of employment, or where it is used as the basis of employment decisions affecting job status or tangible employment benefits. As its name suggests, this form of harassment involves actual or potential economic loss—e.g. termination, transfer, or adverse performance ratings, etc.— as a consequence of the employee's refusal to exchange sexual favors demanded by a supervisor or employer for employment benefits. The second form of actionable harassment consists of unwelcome sexual conduct that is of such severity as to alter a condition of employment by creating an "intimidating, hostile or offensive working environment." The essence of a "hostile environment" claim is a "pattern or practice" of offensive behavior by the employer, a supervisor, co-workers, or non-employees so "severe or pervasive" as to interfere with the employee's job performance or create an abusive work environment.

In 1980, the federal agency responsible for enforcing Title VII issued interpretative guidelines prohibiting both *quid pro quo* and hostile environment sexual harassment. The EEOC guidelines focus on sexuality

---

[8] 42 U.S.C. Sec. 4000e-2(a)(1).

[9] 42 U.S.C. 2000 et seq. Sexual harassment in federally assisted education programs is also prohibited by Title IX of the 1972 Education Amendments. 20 U.S.C. Sec. 1681 et seq. (Franklin v. Gwinnet County Public Schools. 503 U.S. 60 (1992)). While Title VII and Title IX are the primary sources of federal sexual harassment law, relief from such conduct has also been sought, albeit less frequently, pursuant to Sec. 1983 of Title 42, the Federal Employees Liability Act, and the Equal Protection and Due Process Clauses of the U.S. Constitution. E.g. Doe v. Taylor Independent School District, 975 F.2d 137 (5th Cir. 1992)(holding that a student has a firmly established equal protection and due process right to be free from sexual molestation by a state-employed school teacher).

rather than gender—in terms of job detriments resulting from "[u]nwelcome sexual advances, requests for sexual favors, and other verbal or physical behavior of a sexual nature"—and require that a "totality of the circumstances" be considered to determine whether particular conduct constitutes sexual harassment.[10] In addition, judicial developments in hostile environment law were anticipated by elimination of tangible economic loss as a factor and by providing that unwelcome sexual conduct violates Title VII whenever it "has the purpose or effect of unreasonably interfering with an individual's work performance or creating an intimidating, hostile, or offensive working environment."

According to the EEOC guidelines, an employer is liable for both forms of sexual harassment when perpetrated by supervisors.[11] The employer, however, is liable for harassment perpetrated by co-worker or non-employees only if the employer knew or should have known of the harassment and failed to "take immediate and appropriate corrective action."[12] They also recommend that employers take preventive measures to eliminate sexual harassment[13] and state that employers may be liable to those denied employment opportunities or benefits given to another employee because of submission to sexual advances.[14]

On March 19, 1990, the EEOC issued "Policy Guidance on Sexual Harassment" to elaborate on certain legal principles set forth in its interpretative guidelines from a decade before.[15] First, the later document reasserts the basic distinction between "quid pro quo" and "hostile environment" and states that an employer "will always be held responsible for acts of *'quid pro quo'* harassment" by a supervisor while hostile environment cases require "careful examination" of whether the harassing supervisor was acting in an 'agency capacity'".[16] On the "welcomeness" issue, the policy guide states that "a contemporaneous complaint or protest" by the victim is an "important" but "not a necessary element of the claim" Instead, the Commission will look to all "objective evidence, rather than subjective, uncommunicated feelings" to "determine whether the victim's conduct is consistent, or inconsistent, with her assertion that the sexual

---

[10] 29 C.F.R. Sec. 1604.11(a)(1995).

[11] Id. at Sec. 1604.11 (c).

[12] Id. at Sec. 1604.11(d)-(e)(1995).

[13] Id. at Sec. 1604.11(f).

[14] Id. at Sec. 1604.11(g).

[15] BNA, FEP Manual 405:6681 et seq.

[16] Id. at 405:6695.

conduct is unwelcome."[17] In determining whether a work environment is hostile, several factors are emphasized:

> (1) whether the conduct was verbal or physical or both; (2) how frequently it was repeated; (3) whether the conduct was hostile or patently offensive; (4) whether the alleged harasser was a co-worker or supervisor; (5) whether others joined in perpetrating the harassment; and (6) whether the harassment was directed at more than one individual.

However, because the alleged misconduct must "substantially interfere" with the victim's job performance. "sexual flirtation or innuendo, even vulgar language that is trivial or merely annoying. would probably not establish a hostile environment."[18] In addition. "the harasser's conduct should be evaluated from the objective standard of a 'reasonable person.'"[19]

QUID PRO QUO HARASSMENT

The earliest judicial challenges involving tangible benefit or *quid pro quo* harassment claims—filed by women who were allegedly fired for resisting sexual advances by their supervisors—were largely unsuccessful. The discriminatory conduct in such cases was deemed to arise from "personal proclivity" of the supervisor rather than "company directed policy that deprived women of employment opportunities." Until the mid-1970's, federal district courts were reluctant either to find a Title VII cause of action or to impose liability on employers who were neither in complicity with, nor had actual knowledge of. quid pro quo harassment by their supervisory employees. An historic turning point came when the federal district court in *Williams v. Saxbe*[20] held for the first time that sexual harassment was discriminatory treatment within the meaning of Title VII because "it created an artificial barrier to employment which was placed before one gender and not the other, despite the fact that both genders were similarly situated."[21] Echoing earlier opinions that an employer is not liable for "interpersonal disputes between employees," the court nonetheless refused to dismiss the complaint since "if [the alleged harassment was a policy or practice of

---

[17] Id. at 405:6686.
[18] Id.
[19] Id.
[20] 413 F. Supp. 654 (D.D.C. 1976).
[21] Id. at 657-58.

plaintiff's supervisor, then it was the agency's policy or practice, which is prohibited by Title VII."[22]

Appellate tribunals in several federal circuits soon began to affirm that *quid pro quo* harassment violates Title VII where "gender is a substantial factor in the discrimination," reversing contrary lower court holdings. For example, Judge Spotswood Robinson, writing for the D.C. Circuit in *Barnes v. Costle*[23] disagreed with "the notion that employment conditions summoning' sexual relations are somehow exempted from the coverage of Title VII" as implied by the decision below. Finding that it was "enough that gender is a factor contributing to the discrimination in a substantial way," Judge Robinson ruled that differential treatment based upon an employee's rejection of her supervisor's sexual advances violated the statute. Similarly, in *Tompkins v. Public Service Electric & Gas Co.*, the Third Circuit reversed the trial court's denial of Title VII protection to all "sexual harassment and sexually motivated assault," finding that where an employee's "status as a female was a motivating factor in the supervisor's conditioning her continued employment on compliance with his sexual demands," actionable quid pro quo harassment had occurred. "[T]o establish a *prima facie* case of *quid pro quo* harassment, a plaintiff must present evidence that she was subject to unwelcome sexual conduct, and that her reaction to that conduct was then used as the basis for decisions affecting the compensation, terms, conditions, or privileges of her employment."[24] And while the loss of a "tangible employment benefit" has most often meant dismissal or demotion, quid pro quo claims may also arise from denial of career advantages—job title, duties or assignments—of less immediate economic impact upon the employee. The Seventh Circuit, for example, has ruled that a tenured professor who was allegedly stripped of her job title and removed from academic committees because she rebuffed the sexual advances of the university provost may have a claim for quid pro quo sexual harassment under Title VII.[25]

The dismissal by Judge Susan Weber Wright of Paula Jones' sexual harassment lawsuit against President Clinton squarely addressed the workplace consequences that must flow from the refusal to submit to an unwelcome sexual advance for the court to find actionable harassment.[26] Plaintiff Jones claimed that her career advancement had repeatedly been

---

[22] Id. at 660-61.

[23] 561 F.2d 983 (D.C. Cir. 1977).

[24] Karibian v. Columbia University , 14 F.3d 773, 777 (2d Cir.), cert. denied, 114 S.Ct. 2693 (1994).

[25] Bryson v. Chicago State University, 96 F.3d 912 (7th Cir. 1996).

[26] Jones v. Clinton, 16 F. Supp. 2d 1054 (E.D. Ark. 1998).

thwarted by her state employer as retribution for rebuffing the former Arkansas Governor. As evidence of "tangible job detriments," Jones alleged that she had been discouraged by supervisors from seeking job promotions or pay increases; that following return from maternity leave, she was transferred to a new position with fewer responsibilities; that she was effectively denied access to grievance procedures available to other sexual harassment victims; and that by physically isolating her directly outside her supervisor's office with little work to do, she was "subjected to hostile treatment having tangible effects." Judge Wright was unconvinced by the record, however, that any threat perceived by Jones during her alleged hotel meeting with the former Governor was so "clear and unambiguous" as to be a quid pro quo conditioning of "concrete job benefits or detriments on compliance with sexual demands." "Refusal" cases like Jones, calling for proof "tangible job detriment" by plaintiffs who resist unwelcome sexual demands,"[27] were distinguished from so-called "submission" cases, where 'in the nature of things, economic harm will not be available to support the claim of the employee who submits to the supervisor's demands."[28]

It was widely anticipated that some further guidance on the essential character of quid pro quo harassment, particularly in relation to Jones' claims against President Clinton, would be forthcoming when the Supreme Court decided *Burlington Industries, Inc. v. Ellerth*.[29] That case involved a former merchandising assistant at Burlington Industries who alleged that she was the subject of repeated boorish and offensive comments and gestures by a division vice-president who implied that her response to his advances would affect her career. *Ellerth* detailed three incidents in which her supervisor's comments could be construed as threats to deny her tangible job benefits. A short time later, she quit her job without informing anyone in authority about the harassment, even though she was aware of Burlington's anti-harassment policy.

The trial court granted the company's motion to dismiss on the grounds that no adverse consequences flowed from the plaintiff's refusal to submit to the alleged advances. The action was reinstated by a *per curiam* decision of

---

[27] E.g., Cram v. Lamson & Sessions Co., 49 F.3d 466 (8th Cir. 1995); Sanders v. Casa View Baptist Church, 134 F.3d 331,339 (5th Cir. 1998) (noting that to withstand summary judgment on quid pro quo claims. plaintiffs were required to produce evidence showing that the harassment complained of affected tangible aspects of their compensation, terms, conditions, or privileges of employment); Gary v. Long. 59 F.3d 1391. 1396 (D.C. Cir. 1995)("[A] supervisor's mere threat or promise of job-related harm or benefits in exchange for sexual favors does not constitute quid pro quo harassment. . . .").

[28] Karibian v. Columbia Univ., supra n. 23, See also Jansen v. Packaging Corp of American, 123 F.2d 490 (7th Cir. 1997).

[29] 118 S.Ct 2257 (1998).

the entire Seventh Circuit holding the employer strictly liable for *quid pro quo* harassment "even if the supervisor's threat does not result in a company act"[30] or actual economic loss. Appellate court rulings from the Eighth[31] and Eleventh[32] Circuits, on the other hand, had during the same period reaffirmed the necessity of proving actual loss of job benefits or a "tangible job detriment" as an element of a *quid pro quo* claim, Squarely presented by *Ellerth*, therefore, was the question of whether sexual advances by a supervisor accompanied by the threatened but not actualized loss of employment or job benefits may render an employer liable for *quid pro quo* harassment.

In fashioning an employer liability rule in *Ellerth*, and the *Faragher* case decided the same day, the Court considered the judicial distinction between *quid pro quo* and environmental harassment to be less important than whether the claim involved a threat that had been "carried out" in fact. Claims based on unfulfilled threats of retaliation were equated by the Court to hostile environment harassment, requiring plaintiff to prove "severe and pervasive" conduct. Under common law agency principles, as applied by the majority, an employer is generally immune from liability for the tortuous conduct of its agent (the harassing supervisor in *Ellerth*), which is deemed to be "outside the scope of employment," unless the wrongdoer is "aided" in the harassment by "the existence of the agency relation." The "aided in the agency relation standard" differentiates supervisory harassment for which an employer may be automatically liable from similar acts committed by mere co-workers. And it is most clearly satisfied in those cases where the harassment culminates in a "tangible employment action." Such actions, according to Justice Kennedy, include instances where the subordinate employee is subjected to "a significant change in employment status, such as hiring, firing, failing to promote, reassignment with significantly different responsibilities, or a decision causing a significant change in benefits" for failing to permit sexual liberties. Since *Ellerth* had not demonstrated that she was the victim of retaliation by her supervisor — in fact, she had been promoted during the period in question there was no tangible detriment for which the employer could be held strictly liable.

Ellerth was remanded, however, for application of an alternative standard of vicarious employer liability formulated by the Court jointly in *Ellerth* and *Faragher* for supervisory harassment cases not involving a "tangible employment action." Under that rule, after the plaintiff proves that

---

[30] 123 F.3d 490, 494 (7th Cir. 1997)(per curiam).

[31] Davis v. City of Sioux City, 115 F.3d 1365 (8th Cir. 1997).

[32] Farley v. American Cast Iron Pipe Co., 115 F.3d 1548 (11th Cir. 1997).

the supervisory misconduct is both "severe and pervasive," the employer may assert as an "affirmative defense" that its actions to prevent and remedy workplace harassment were "reasonable," while the plaintiff "unreasonably" failed to take advantage of any anti-harassment policies and procedures of the employer. *Ellerth's* failure to avail herself of the employer's grievance procedure likely defeats any Title VII recovery against Burlington under the second prong of this defense. The judicial task for lower courts after *Ellerth* is to construe this duty of reasonable care governing the employer's affirmative defense to liability. Other than rewarding employers for prophylactic measures aimed at workplace harassment and compelling victim participation in those efforts, *Ellerth* provides little specific guidance. Note also that Justice Kennedy's opinion for the majority in *Ellerth* included a passing elliptical reference to *Jones v. Clinton* when it "express[ed] no opinion as to whether a single unfulfilled threat is sufficient to constitute discrimination in the terms or conditions of employment." This *dictum* largely begs the district court's conclusion that harassing circumstances alleged by Jones did not create a hostile environment, and since no "tangible employment action" was proven, any finding of actionable harassment under federal law was unwarranted.

Hostile Environment Harassment

The earlier judicial focus on economic detriment or *quid pro quo* harassment—making submission to sexual demands a condition to job benefits—largely gave way to Title VII claims for harassment that creates an "intimidating, hostile, or offensive environment." The first federal appellate court to jettison the tangible economic loss requirement and recognize a hostile environment claim of sexual harassment was the D.C. Circuit in *Bundy v. Jackson.*[33] The plaintiff there charged that several supervisors made continual sexual advances and propositions, questioned her about her sexual proclivities, ignored her complaints, criticized her work performance, and attempted to block her bid for promotion. The appeals court ruled that actionable sex discrimination is not limited to gender-based conditions resulting in a tangible job consequence, but occurs whenever sex is a motivating factor in treating an employee in an adverse manner. Despite the plaintiffs failure to prove *quid pro quo* harassment—she was not fired, demoted, or denied a promotion—the court was unwilling to adopt a rule

---

[33] 641 F.2d 934 (1981).

that would permit an employer to lawfully harass an employee "by carefully stopping short of firing the employee or taking any other tangible actions against her in response to her resistance."[34] Another decision important to the judicial development of sexually hostile environment law was *Henson v. Dundee* where the Eleventh Circuit rejected a claim of *quid pro quo* harassment but found that the employee had a right to a trial on the merits to determine whether the misconduct alleged made her job environment hostile.[35]

Mentor Savings Bank v. Vinson[36] ratified the consensus then emerging among the federal circuits by recognizing a Title VII cause of action for sexual harassment. Writing for the Supreme Court in 1986, then-Justice Rehnquist affirmed that a "hostile environment," predicated on "purely psychological aspects of the workplace environment," could give rise to legal liability and that "tangible loss" of "an economic character" was not an essential element. This holding was qualified by the Court with important reservations drawn from earlier administrative and judicial precedent. First, "not all workplace conduct that can be described as 'harassment' affects a term condition, or privilege of employment within the meaning of Title VII." For example, the "mere utterance" of an "epithet" engendering "offensive feelings in an employee" would not ordinarily be per se actionable, the opinion suggests. Rather, the misconduct "must be sufficiently severe or pervasive to alter the conditions of [the victim's] employment and create an abusive working environment."[37]

---

[34] Id. at 945.

[35] 682 F.2d 897 (11th Cir. 1982). In an oft-quoted passage from its opinion, the court stated:

> Sexual harassment which creates a hostile or offensive environment for members of one sex is every bit the arbitrary barrier to sexual equality at the workplace that racial harassment is to racial equality. Surely, a requirement that a man or woman run a gauntlet of sexual abuse in return for the privilege of being allowed to work and make a living can be as demeaning and disconcerting as the harshest of racial epithets. A pattern of sexual harassment inflicted upon an employee because of her sex is a pattern of behavior that inflicts disparate treatment upon a member of one sex with respect to terms, conditions, or privileges of employment. There is no requirement that an employee subjected to such disparate treatment prove in addition that she suffered tangible job detriment. Id. at 902, 477 U.S. 57 (1986).

[36] 477 U.S. 57 (1986).

[37] Id. at 62 (quoting Henson v. Dundee), supra n. 21 at 904, In Vinson the complainant alleged that her supervisor demanded sexual relations over a three-year period, fondled her in front of other employees, followed her into the women's restroom and exposed himself to her, and forcibly raped her several times. She claimed she submitted for fear of jeopardizing her employment. During the period she received several promotions, which, it was undisputed, were based on merit alone so that no exchange of job advancement for sexual favors (quid pro quo harassment) was alleged or found.

Second, while "voluntariness" in the sense of consent is not a defense to a sexual harassment charge,

> [t]he gravamen of any sexual harassment claim is that the alleged sexual advances were 'unwelcome.' . . .The correct inquiry is whether respondent by her conduct indicated that the alleged sexual advances were unwelcome, not whether her actual participation in sexual intercourse was voluntary.[38]

Accordingly, "it does not follow that a complainant's sexually provocative speech or dress is irrelevant as a matter of law in determining whether he or she found particular sexual advances unwelcome. To the contrary, such evidence is obviously relevant."[39]

Finally, turning to the issue of employer liability, the *Vinson* majority held that the court below had "erred in concluding that employers are always automatically liable for sexual harassment by their supervisors."[40] The usual rule in Title VII cases is strict liability, and four Justices, concurring in the judgment, argued that the same rule should apply in the sexual harassment context as well. The majority disagreed, impliedly suggesting that in hostile environment cases no employer, at least none with a formal policy against harassment, should he made liable in the absence of actual or constructive knowledge.[41]

The Supreme Court's failure to clearly define what constitutes a hostile environment in *Mentor Saving* led to frequent conflict in the lower courts. For example, three federal Circuit Courts of Appeals—the Sixth, the Seventh, and the Eleventh—concluded that in a sexual harassment case, a plaintiff must not only prove that the conduct complained of would have offended a reasonable victim and that he or she was actually offended, but also that the plaintiff suffered serious psychological injury as a result of the conduct.[42] On the other hand, three other Circuits, the Third, the Eighth, and the Ninth, held that the Title VII plaintiff need demonstrate only that he or

---

[38] Id. at 68 (citing 29 C.F.R Sec. 1604.11(a)(1985)).

[39] Id. at 69.

[40] Id. at 72.

[41] On the issue of employer liability, Meritor states:

> [While] declin[ing] the parties' invitation to issue a definitive rule on employer liability. . . we do agree with the EEOC that Congress wanted courts to look to agency principles for guidance in this area. While such common-law principles may not be transferable in all their particulars to Title VII, Congress' decision to define 'employer' to include any agent' of an employer, 42 U.S.C. § 2000e(b). surely evinces an intent to place some limits on the acts of employees for which employers under Title VII arc to be held responsible. Id. at 72-73.

[42] Rabidue v. Osceola Refining Co., 805 F.2d 611 (6th Cir. 1986); Scott v. Sears Roebuck, 798 F.2d 210 (7th Cir. 1986); and Brooms v. Regal Tube, 830 F. 2d 1554 (11th Cir. 1987).

she was actually offended by conduct that would be deemed offensive by a reasonable victim.[43]

Harris v. Forklift Systems, Inc.[44] revisited and offered some clarification of *Meritor Savings*. The Supreme Court granted certiorari in *Harris* to resolve the conflict among the circuits over whether harassing conduct must produce severe psychological harm to create an actionable hostile environment under Title VII. A company president had subjected a female manager to sexual innuendo, unwanted physical touching, and insults because of her gender. After two years, she left the job. Despite its determination that demeaning sexual comments by the employer had "offended the plaintiff, and would offend the reasonable woman," the trial court ruled against the plaintiff since the conduct alleged was not "so severe as to be expected to seriously affect plaintiff's psychological well-being" or create an "intimidating or abusive" environment. the Sixth Circuit upheld the trial court ruling in a three-paragraph unpublished opinion.

The Supreme Court reversed, deciding in 1993 that hostile environment sexual harassment need not "seriously affect psychological well-being" of the victim before Title VII is violated. *Meritor Savings*, wrote Justice O'Connor, had adopted a "middle path" between condemning conduct that was "merely offensive" and requiring proof of "tangible psychological injury." Thus, a hostile environment is not created by the "mere utterance of an ... epithet which engenders offensive feelings in an employee.'" On the other hand, a victim of sexual harassment need not experience a "nervous breakdown" for the law to come into play. "So long as the environment would reasonably be perceived, and is perceived, as hostile or abuse, there is no need for it also to be psychologically injurious."

Harris also addressed the standard of reasonableness to be applied in judging sexual harassment claims, an issue dividing the lower federal courts then and now. Justice O'Connor opted for a two-part analysis, both components of which must be met for a violation to be found. First, the conduct must create an objectively hostile work environment - "an environment that a reasonable person would find hostile and abusive." Second, the victim must subjectively perceive the environment to be abusive. The "totality of circumstances" surrounding the alleged harassment are to guide judicial inquiry, including "the frequency of the discriminatory conduct; its severity; whether it is physically threatening or humiliating or a

---

[43] Andrews v. City of Philadelphia, 895 F.2d 1469 (3d Cir. 1990); Burns v. McGregor Electronic Industries, Inc., 955 F.2d 559 (8th Cir. 1992); and Ellison v. Brady, 924 F.2d 872 (9th Cir. 1991).

[44] 510 U.S. 17 (1993).

mere offensive utterance; and whether it unreasonably interferes with an employee's work performance." Significantly, however, *Harris* did not explicitly resolve a fundamental issue raised by several lower courts regarding the appropriate "gender perspective" to consider in assessing sexual harassment claims.[45]

An increasingly broad range of hostile environment harms—frequently as concerned with lewd comments, inquiries, jokes or displays of pornographic materials in the workplace as with overt sexual aggression— have been brought before the federal courts. *Robinson v. Jackson Shipyards, Inc.*[46] was among the first reported decisions to impose liability for sexual harassment based on the pervasive presence of

sexually oriented materials—magazine foldouts or other pictorial depictions—and "sexually demeaning remarks and jokes" by male co-workers without allegations of physical assaults or sexual propositions directed at the plaintiff Most courts, however, have limited recovery to cases involving repeated sexual demands or other offensive conduct.[47] Except for cases involving touching or extreme verbal behavior, courts are often reluctant to find that sexual derision—or claims against pornography in the workplace—when unaccompanied by sexual demands, is sufficient to create

---

[45] Compare, e.g. Rabidue v. Osceola Refining Co., 805 F.2d 611, 622 (6th Cir. 1986)(holding that barrage of "nudie" pictures and litany of degrading comments were "annoying." but would not be sufficiently offensive to a reasonable person so as to interfere with the person's work performance), cert. denied, 481 U.S. 1041 (1987) with Robinson v. Jacksonville Shipyards. Inc.. 760 F. Supp. 1486, 1524 (M.D. Fla. l991)(applying reasonable woman standard to determine that pervasive pornographic pictures, sexual comments, verbal harassment, abusive graffiti, and unwelcome touching of some of plaintiffs female co-workers created a hostile working environment) and Spenser v. General Electric Co., 697 F. Supp. 204, 218 (E.D. Va.1988)(finding that sexual comments and suggestive behavior of plaintiffs superior, such as sitting on female workers' laps and talking about private parts, would have seriously affected the psychological well-being of reasonable female employee), aff'd, 894 F.2d 651 (4th Cir. 1990). See also Ellison v. Brady. 924 F.2d 872, 879 (9th Cir. 1991)(adopting reasonable woman standard).

[46] 760 F.Supp. 1486 (M.D. Fla. 1991).

[47] E.g. Highlander v. K.F.C. Nat'l Management Co., 805 F. 2d 644 (6th Cir. 1986)(holding that one instance of fondling and one verbal proposition were not sufficient to establish "hostile environment"); Eg. Waltman v. Int'l Paper Co., 875 F.2d 468. 475 (5th Cir. 1989)("focus is whether [plaintiff] was subjected to recurring acts of discrimination, not whether a given individual harassed [plaintiff] recurrently,"); King v. Board of Regents, 898 F.2d 533, 537 (7th Cir. 1990)("although a single act can be enough. . . generally repeated incidents create a stronger claim of hostile environment, with the strength of the claim depending on the number of incidents and the intensity of each incident"). But cf. Vance v. Southern Tel. & Tel. Co., 863 F.2d 1503. 1510 (11th Cir. 1989)("the determination of whether the defendant's conduct is sufficiently severe or pervasive' to constitute racial harassment does not turn solely on the number of incidents alleged by plaintiff.").

a hostile environment.[48] This tendency may be reinforced by the Court's admonition in *Oncale* that Congress never intended Title VII to become a general "code of civility." But conduct need not be overtly sexual; other hostile conduct directed against the victim because of the victim's sex is also prohibited.[49] And, in line with *Vinson*, evidence of a sexual harassment claimant's own provocative behavior or prior workplace conduct is generally relevant to a judicial determination of whether the defendant's conduct was unwelcome.[50]

Claims involving isolated or intermittent incidents have frequently been dismissed as insufficiently pervasive.[51] In Jones v. Clinton[52], for example.

---

[48] For example, in Hall v. Gus Construction Cc., 842 F.2d 1010, 1017 (8th Cir. 1988), having found that defendants' conduct had gone "far beyond that which even the least sensitive of persons is expected to tolerate," the Eighth Circuit nonetheless felt compelled to add that "Title VII does not mandate an employment environment worthy of a Victorian salon. Nor do we expect that our holding today will displace all ribaldry on the roadway." See also Cowan v. Prudential ins. Co. of America, 141 F.3d 751, 758 (7th Cir. 1998)(no hostile environment where offensive comments were "fairly sporadic . . . [and] unrelated incidents which occurred over two years of [plaintiff's] employment, were not physically threatening, most of the incidents were not severe, and only two of the incidents were directed at plaintiff'); Jones v. Flagship Int'l, 793 F.2d 714 (5th Cir. 1986)(holding that two requests for sexual contact plus one incident of bare-breasted mermaids as table decorations for a company party were insufficiently pervasive to create hostile environment), cert. denied. 479 U.S. 1065 (1987).

[49] See Williams v. General Motors Corp., F.3d (6th Cir, 1999); Andrews v. City of Philadelphia. 898 F.2d 1469. 1485 (3d Cir. 1990)("The Supreme Court [in Vinson] in no way limited this concept to intimidation or ridicule of an explicitly sexual nature."); Bell v. Crackin Good Bakers, Inc., 777 F.2d 1497, 1503 (11th Cir. 1985)(holding that valid claim could be based on "threatening. bellicose, demeaning, hostile, or offensive conduct by a supervisor in the workplace because of the sex of the victim"); McKinney v. Dole, 765 F.2d 1129, 1140 (D.C.Cir. 1985)(district court erred in assuming that incident of physical force could not constitute sexual harassment unless "explicitly sexual").

[50] See, e.g., Jones v. Wesco Investments Inc., 846 F.2d 1154 n.5 (8th Cir. 1988)("A court must consider any provocative speech or dress of the plaintiff in a sexual harassment case."); Swentek v. USAIR, Inc., 830 F.2d 552. 556 (4th Cir. 1987)(affirming trial judge's determination to permit testimony that the plaintiff was "a foul-mouthed individual who often talked about sex," that the plaintiff had placed a "dildo in her supervisor's mailbox" and once grabbed the genitals of a male co-worker and sexually propositioned him).

[51] Sousa v. Nestle USA Company, 181 F.3d 958 (8~ Cir. 1999)(pattern of co-worker harassment not actionable because it was not so severe or pervasive as to prevent plaintiff from performing all her duties on a full-time basis); Lam v. Curators of the Univ. of Mo,, 122 F.3d 654. 656-57 (8th Cir. 1997)(noting that single exposure to offensive videotape was not severe or pervasive enough to create hostile environment); Sprague v. Thorn Americas, Inc. 129 F.3d 1355. 1366 (7th Cir. l997)(five sexually-oriented incidents spread out over the course of 16 months not sufficiently severe or pervasive to create hostile environment); Saxton v. American Tel. & Tel. Co., 10 F.3d 526, 534 (7~ Cir. 1993)("relatively limited" instances of unwanted sexual advances, which included the supervisor placing his hand on plaintiffs leg above the knee several times, rubbing his hand along her upper thigh; kissing her several seconds, and "lurching at her from behind some bushes," did not create an objectively hostile work environment); Chamberlin v. 101 Realty. 915 F.2d 777 (1st Cir. 1990)(five mild sexual advances by a supervisor. without more, were insufficient);

Judge Wright ruled that considering the "totality of circumstances," an alleged hotel incident and other encounters between Paula Jones and former Governor Clinton were not "the kind of sustained and nontrivial conduct necessary for a claim of hostile work environment." In particular, the court noted that plaintiff Jones "never missed a day of work" because of the incident nor did she complain to her supervisors; never did she seek medical or psychological treatment as a consequence of alleged harassment; and that her allegations generally failed to demonstrate any adverse workplace effects. The Seventh Circuit, in another case, concluded that while an Illinois state employee "subjectively perceived her work environment to he hostile and abusive" the paucity of sexually oriented comments complained of— three suggestive comments by a co-worker over a three-month period— "were not sufficiently severe that a reasonable person would feel subjected to a hostile working environment."[53] Of course, a single incident may be actionable if it is linked to a granting or denial of an employment benefit (*quid pro quo* harassment),[54] or if the incident involves physical assault[55] or touching of the employee in an offensive manner under circumstances that preclude her escape.[56] The EEOC policy statement also states that the agency "will presume that the unwelcome, intentional touching of a charging party's

---

Drinkwater v. Union Carbide Corp., 904 F.2d 853 (3d Cir. 1990)(a claim must demonstrate a "continuous period of harassment and two comments do not create an atmosphere."); Ebert v. Lamar Truck Plaza, 878 F.2d 338 (10th Cir. 1989)(use of foul language and infrequent touching of employees at 24-hour restaurant was not pervasive or severe and management promptly took corrective action whenever complaints were made).

[52] Supra n. 25.

[53] McKensie v. Illinois Department of Transportation. 92 F.3d 473 (7th Cir. 1996). See also Butler v. Ysleta Independent School District, 161 F.3d 263 (5th Cir. 1998) (sexually offensive messages anonymously sent by elementary school principal to two female teachers not actionable since they were infrequent and non-threatening and were received at home while it is the "workplace itself [that] is central to the wrong of sexual harassment." Penry v. Federal Home Loan Bank of Topeka, 155 F.3d 1257 (10th Cir. 1998)(gender-based inappropriate behavior of supervisor over a three-year period— including needless touching, grabbing, and offensive comments—evinced "poor taste and lack of professionalism,' but incidents "were too few and far between to be considered" harassment). But cf, Abeita v. TransAmerica Mailings, 159 F.3d 246 (6th Cir. 1998)(though not directed at plaintiff, supervisor's sexually provocative statements to her about other women for an ongoing and continual basis for seven years, were sufficiently severe and pervasive to send case to the jury).

[54] Neville v. Taft Broadcasting Co., 857 F. Supp. 1461 (W.D.N.Y. 1987).

[55] Crisonino v. New York City Housing Auth., 985 F. Supp. 385 (S.D.N.Y. 1997)(supervisor called plaintiff a 'dumb bitch" and 'shoved her so hard that she fell backward and hit the floor, sustaining injuries from which she has vet to fully recover").

[56] Davis v. U.S. Postal Service, 142 r.3d 1334 (10th Cir. 1998) ("[a] rational jury could find that a work environment in which a plaintiff is subjected to regular unwelcome hugging and kissing combined with other specific incidents . . . [including] an assault. is objectively hostile.").

intimate body areas is sufficiently offensive to alter the conditions of her working environment and constitute a violation of Title VII."[57]

SAME-SEX HARASSMENT

Title VII was interpreted early on by the courts and the EEOC to protect both men and women against workplace sexual harassment by the opposite sex. In *Meritor*, the Court found that Congress intended "to strike at the entire spectrum of disparate treatment of men and women" in employment and read Title VII to prohibit discriminatory harassment by a supervisor "because of the subordinate's sex." Until the Supreme Court decision in *Oncale Sundowner Offshore Services, Inc.*, however federal courts were sharply divided over whether the Ad applied when the harasser and the victim are of the same sex. Although Title VII does not prohibit direct discrimination by an employer based on an employee's sexual orientation[58]—whether homosexual, bisexual, or heterosexual—the EEOC[59] and the District of Columbia,[60] Sixth,[61] Seventh,[62] Eighth,[63] Ninth Circuit,[64]

---

[57] BNA, FEP Manual at 405:6681.

[58] Ulane v. Eastern Airlines, Inc., 742 F.2d 1081 (7th Cir. 1984), cert. denied, 471 U.S. 1017 (1985).

[59] The EEOC. Compliance Manual states that the respective sexes of the harasser and the victim are irrelevant in determining whether Title VII has been violated:

The victim does not have to be of the opposite sex from the harasser. Since sexual harassment is a form of sex discrimination, the crucial inquiry is whether the harasser treats a member or members of one sex differently from members of the other sex. The victim and the harasser may be of the same sex where, for instance, the sexual harassment is based on the victim's sex (not on the victim's sexual preference) and the harasser does not treat the employees of the sex the same way.

EEOC Compliance Manual, Sec. 615.2(b)(3). While EEOC interpretations of Title VII are not binding on the courts, they are frequently accorded judicial deference, See Mentor, 477 U.S. at 65.

[60] Barnes v. Costle, 561 F.2d 983, 990 n. 55 (D.C.Cir. 1977)(acluio~v1edging the possibility of actionable Title VII claim where "a subordinate of either gender" is harassed "by a homosexual superior of the same gender.").

[61] Yeary v. Goodwill Industries—Knoxville. Inc., 107 F.3d 443 (6th Cir. 1997) ("It is not necessary for this court to decide today whether same-sex harassment can be actionable only when the harasser is homosexual; all that is necessary for us to observe is that when a male sexually propositions another male because of sexual attraction, there can be little question that the behavior is a form of harassment that occurs because the propositioned male is male—that is 'because of. sex.'")

[62] Baskerville v. Culligan Int'l Co., 50 F.3d 428, 430 (7th Cir. 1995) (In a heterosexual harassment action, the court noted parenthetically that "sexual harassment of women by men is the most common kind, but we do not mean to exclude the possibility that sexual harassment of men by women, or men by other men, or women by other women would not

and Eleventh Circuits[65] all indicated that same-sex harassment was actionable in some circumstances. An apparent majority of federal district courts to consider the issue also allowed such claims where the alleged harassment is "because of" the victim's sex;[66] the rationale being that Title VII bars disparate treatment based on the sex or gender of the employee, without regard to whether the harasser is male or female. Nonetheless, the Fifth Circuit concluded with minimal analysis that same sex harassment was never actionable,[67] while other courts had limited Title VII liability to same sex cases based on homosexual conduct since only then was the harassment deemed to be "because of sex."[68]

On March 4, 1998, the U.S. Supreme Court entered the fray and while providing a modicum of specific guidance, agreed with the majority view of the federal courts that "nothing in Title VII necessarily bars a claim of discrimination 'because of sex' merely because the plaintiff and defendant (or the person charged with acting on behalf of the defendant) are of the same sex." *Oncale v. Sundowner Offshore Services, Inc.*[69] involved *quid pro*

---

be actionable in appropriate cases."). See also J. Doe & H. Doe v. City of Belleville, 119 F.3d 563 (7th Cir. 1997).

[63] Quick v. Donaldson Co., 90 F.3d 1372 (8th Cir. 1996)(evidence that male employees were the sole targets of other heterosexuals who practiced "bagging" co-worker testicles could lead to finding that such treatment was based on sex).

[64] Steiner v. Showboat Operating Co.. 25 F.3d 1459, 1464 (9th Cir. 1994)(commenting that "we do not rule out the possibility that both men and women... have viable claims against [a male supervisor] for sexual harassment"), cert. denied 115 S. Ct. 733 (1995).

[65] Fredette v. BVP Management Associates, 112 F.3d 1503 (11th Cir. 1997)("when homosexual male supervisor solicits sexual favors from a male subordinate and conditions work benefits or detriment on receiving such favors, the male subordinate can state a viable Title VII claim for gender discrimination").

[66] See Gerd v. United Parcel Service. Inc., 934 F. Supp. 357 (D.Colo. 1996) and cases cited therein.

[67] Garcia v. Elf Atochem North America, 28 F.3d 449 (5th Cir. 1994) denied that "harassment by a male supervisor against a male subordinate [states] a claim under Title VII even though the harassment has sexual overtones" based on the earlier Fifth Circuit ruling in Goluszek v. Smith. The Goluszek court refused "a wooden application" of Title VII to salvage same-sex claims in favor of an interpretation that focused on "imbalance" and "abuse" of power in the workplace directed at "discrete and vulnerable groups." Title VII claims were limited, said the court, to the "exploitation of a powerful position to impose sexual demands or pressures on an unwilling but less powerful person." Since a male in a "male dominated" work environment was not "inferior"— or a victim of a "gender-biased atmosphere; an atmosphere of oppression by a 'dominant gender'"—same sex harassment was not actionable. See also Vandevanter v. Wabash Nat'l Corp., 867 F. Supp. 790 (N.D.Ind. 1994).

[68] McWilliams v. Board of Supervisors, 72 F.3d 1191 (4th Cir. 1996). See also Wrightson v. Pizza Hut of America, inc. 99 F.3d 138 (4th Cit. 1996)("a claim may lie under Title VII for same-sex hostile work environment sexual harassment where, as here, the individual charged with the discrimination is homosexual").

[69] 118 S.Ct 998 (1998).

quo and hostile environment claims of a male offshore oil rig worker who alleged that he was sexually assaulted and abused by his supervisor and two male co-workers for three months in 1991, forcing him to quit his job. Relying on the Fifth Circuit's earlier Garcia ruling, a federal judge in Louisiana dismissed the action. On appeal, the Fifth Circuit observed that Title VII's prohibition against sex discrimination is "gender-neutral" and seemed persuaded by *Meritor* and *Harris* that "so long as the plaintiff proves that harassment is because of the victim's sex, the sex of the harasser and victim is irrelevant." Nonetheless, the appeals court viewed itself bound by the panel decision in Garcia, which could not be overruled, absent a contrary en banc ruling by the Fifth Circuit or superceding decision by the Supreme Court.

In a remarkably brief opinion, the Supreme Court revived *Oncale's* federal lawsuit, voting unanimously to defeat "a categorical rule excluding same-sex harassment claims from the coverage of Title VII." Long on implication, but short on detail, Justice Scalia's opinion for the court is notable for its emphasis on general sexual harassment principles— transcending the limits of the same-sex issue before the Court—and possibly paving the way for stricter scrutiny of sexual harassment claims in general. First, the opinion observes that federal discrimination laws do not prohibit "all verbal or physical harassment in the workplace," only conduct that is discriminatory and based on sex. Moreover, harassing or offensive conduct "is not automatically discrimination because of sex, merely because the words used have a sexual content or connotation." instead, Justice Scalia emphasized, those alleging harassment must prove that the conduct was not just offensive, hut "actually constituted" discrimination. Secondly, reiterating Mentor and Harris, only conduct so "severe or pervasive" and objectively offensive as to alter the conditions of the victim's employment is actionable so that "courts and juries do not mistake ordinary socializing in the workplace—such as male-on-male horseplay or intersexual flirtation— for discriminatory conditions of employment. "'Another modulating aspect of the *Oncale* ruling is the Court's obvious concern for "social context" and workplace realities when appraising all sexual harassment claims—same-sex or otherwise.

> The real social impact of workplace behavior often depends on a constellation of surrounding circumstances, expectations, and relationships which are not fully captured by a simple recitation of the words used or the physical acts performed. Common sense and an appropriate sensitivity to social context, will enable courts and juries to distinguish between simple teasing or roughhousing among members of the same sex, and conduct

which a reasonable person in the plaintiff's position would find severely hostile or abusive.

The net effect of *Oncale* for same sex harassment and hostile environment cases generally is difficult to predict. The Court clearly reinjected the element of discrimination — "because of sex" — back into harassment law, perhaps tempering a tendency on the part of some lower courts to equate offensive behavior with a hostile environment without more, indeed, Justice Scalia goes so far as to state that "Title VII does not prohibit all verbal or physical harassment" and "requires neither asexuality or androgyny in the workplace." Because little guidance is offered, however, for determining when untoward conduct crosses the line to sex-based discrimination, formidable obstacles may remain for Joseph Oncale, the victor before the Supreme Court, and others like hint Justice Scalia's opinion suggests two possible approaches to demonstrating a nexus between sexually offensive conduct and gender discrimination.

> A trier of fact might reasonably find such discrimination, for example, if a female victim is harassed in such sex-specific and derogatory terms by another woman as to make it clear that the harasser is motivated by general hostility to the presence of women in the workplace. A same-sex harassment plaintiff may also, of course, offer direct comparative evidence about how the alleged harasser treated members of both sexes in a mixed-sex workplace.

But it is difficult to discern how either approach would aid male same-sex plaintiffs like *Oncale* in proving discrimination "because of sex" when they are victims of harassment by other males on an oil rig or in other male-dominated workplaces.

The *Oncale* ruling may also mark a general tempering of earlier decisions driving current trends in sexual harassment litigation. The numerous examples of "innocuous differences" in the way men and women interact cited by the Court might serve as the basis for future judicial acceptance of a wider latitude of behavior in the workplace than might otherwise have been considered permissible. The lengths to which Justice Scalia seems to go in articulating the bounds of permissible heterosexual behavior in a same-sex harassment case reinforces this conclusion. Thus, the express approval of "intersexual flirtation" and "teasing or roughhousing" implies that a certain level of fraternization in the workplace is permissible and the consequent range of actionable conduct correspondingly reduced. In this regard, the decision's emphasis upon "social context" may complicate the already difficult judicial task of identifying a sexually hostile work environment. Does this mean, for example, that conduct permitted in a blue-collar workplace may be actionable in a white-collar, professional environment? Thus, the decision might lead to the dismissal of cases the courts have entertained in the past. At the very least, beyond its threshold endorsement of a same-sex cause of action under Title VII, the *Oncale* decision appears to raise as many questions as it answers.

REMEDIES

One major aspect of the 1991 Civil Rights Act[70] of particular importance to sexual harassment claimants was the extension of jury trials and compensatory and punitive damages as remedies for Title VII violations. Previously, Title VII plaintiffs had no right to a jury trial and were entitled only to equitable relief in the form of injunctions against future employer misconduct, reinstatement, and limited backpay for any loss of income resulting from any discharge, denial of promotion, or other adverse employment decision. Consequently, victims of alleged sexual harassment were often compelled to rely on state fair employment practices laws,[71] or traditional common law causes of action for assault, intentional infliction of emotional distress, unlawful interference with contract, invasion of privacy, and the like, to obtain complete monetary relief.[72] Section 102 of the 1991 Act[73] altered the focus of federal EEO enforcement from reliance on judicial injunctions, where voluntary conciliation efforts fail, to jury trials, and compensatory and punitive damages, in Title VII actions involving intentional discrimination.

Compensatory damages under the 1991 Act include "future pecuniary losses, emotional pain, suffering, inconvenience, mental anguish, loss of enjoyment of life, and other non-pecuniary losses."[74] The compensatory and punitive damages provided by Sec. 102 are "in addition to any relief authorized by Section 706(g)" of the 1964 Civil Rights Act.[75] Therefore, plaintiffs may recover damages in addition to equitable relief, including

---

[70] Pub. L. 102-166, 105 Stat. 1071.

[71] E.g., Wirig v. Kinney Shoe Corp., 448 N.W. 2d 526, 51 FEP Cases 885 (Minn. Ct. App. 1989), aff'd in part and rev'd in part on other grounds, 461 N.W.2d 374 (Minn. Sup.Ct. 1990).

[72] See e.g. Rojo v. Kliger, 52 Cal.2d 65, 901 P.2d 373 (Cal. Sup. Ct. 1990); Baker v. Weyerhauser Co., 903 F.2d 1342 (10th Cir. 1990); Syndex Corp. v. Dean, 820 S.W.2d 869 (Tex. App. 1991).

[73] 105 Stat. 1072, 42 U.S.C. Sec. 1981a.

[74] 42 U.S.C. Sec. 1981a(b)(3).

[75] Id. at Sec. 1981a(a)(1).

backpay. Punitive damages may also be recovered against private employers where the plaintiff can demonstrate that the employer acted "with malice or reckless indifference" to the individual's federally protected rights. Punitive damages are not recoverable, however, against a governmental entity.[76] In cases where a plaintiff seeks compensatory or punitive damages, any party may demand a jury trial.[77]

The damages remedy under the Act is limited by dollar amount, however, according to the size of the defendant employer during the twenty or more calendar weeks in the current or preceding calendar year. The sum of compensatory and punitive damages awarded may not exceed $50,000 in the case of an employer with more than 14 and fewer than 101 employees; $100,000 in the case of an employer with more than 100 and fewer 201 employees; $200,000 in the case of an employer with more than 200 and fewer than 501 employees; and $300,000 in the case of an employer with more than 500 employees.[78] In jury trial cases, the court may not inform the jury of the damage caps set forth in the statute.

A recent ruling by the Ninth Circuit Court of Appeals significantly increases the amount of damages that may be awarded a former employee who proves harassment or other intentional discrimination based on race, color, religion, sex, or national origin under Title VII, or disability under the Americans with Disability Act. The trial judge and jury in *Gotthardt v National Railroad*[79] awarded $350,000 in compensatory damages and $124,010.46 back pay for lost wages to a 59-year-old woman who was forced to quit her job due to posttraumatic stress syndrome caused by workplace harassment. Because she claimed that her age, stress, and background would foreclose a future job or career, the trial court also awarded the employee more than $600,000 in "front pay" to cover wages lost from the date of jury verdict forward for eleven years. Amtrak argued that this front pay award must be included in the $300,000 statutory cap on damages as "future pecuniary losses" specifically covered by the statute. Unfortunately for employers, however, the Ninth Circuit determined that front pay is an equitable remedy, rather than legal damages, and therefore not subject to the cap. There is currently a division in the federal circuits on this issue, but until the Supreme Court finally resolves the dispute, the stakes for employers may be considerable. The estimated monetary values of pending cases may be multiplied several times if juries or judges can be

---

[76] Id. at Sec. 1981a(b)(I).
[77] Id. at Sec. 1981a(c).
[78] Id. at Sec. 1981a(b)(3).
[79] 191 F.3d 1148 (9th Cir. 1999).

persuaded by plaintiffs' attorneys to award front pay for years, or even decades, into the future.

The expansion of Title 711 remedies dramatically affects the level of relief available in cases of intentional sex discrimination, where for the first time employees in the private sector have the prospect of federal compensatory and punitive damage recoveries and the right to a jury trial. The Act now provides a monetary remedy for victims of sexual harassment in employment in addition to lost wages. Since harassment of the hostile environment type often occurs without economic loss to the employee, in terms of pay or otherwise, critics of the prior law charged that the sexual harassment victim was frequently without any effective federal relief Title VII plaintiffs may now seek monetary compensation for emotional pain and suffering, and other pecuniary and non-pecuniary losses, caused by sexual harassment. Moreover, federal claims may be joined with pendent state-law claims for damages unlimited by the caps in the federal law or an election made between pursuing state and federal remedies.

LIABILITY OF EMPLOYERS AND SUPERVISORS FOR MONETARY DAMAGES

The addition of monetary damages to the arsenal of Title VII remedies rekindled inquiry into an employer's liability for harassment perpetrated by its supervisors and non-supervisory employees, and of the personal liability of individual harassers, The *Ellerth* decision ratified the federal circuit courts, which had generally declared employers vicariously liable for *quid pro quo* sexual harassment committed by supervisors[80] culminating in tangible job detriment. Only those with actual authority to hire, promote, discharge or affect the terms and conditions of employment can engage in *quid pro quo* harassment and are held to act as agents of the employer, regardless of their motivations. *Quid pro quo* harassment is viewed no differently than other forms of discrimination prohibited by Title VII, for which employers have routinely been held vicariously liable. Because Title VII defines employer to include any agent" of the employer, the statute is understood to have incorporated the principle of *respondeat superior*, in effect holding "employers liable for the discriminatory [acts of]. . . supervisory employees whether or not the employer knew, should have

---

[80] See Horn v. Duke Homes, 755 F.2d 599, 604 (7th Cir. 1985) (noting that all circuits reaching the issue have held employers strictly liable for quid pro quo harassment.

known, or approved of the supervisor's actions.[81] "However, the suggestion in *Mentor Savings Bank* that courts look to agency law in developing liability rules for hostile work environment led most lower federal courts to reject vicarious liability for employers lacking actual or constructive knowledge of environmental harassment perpetrated by a supervisor.

Prior to *Ellerth* and *Faragher*, most courts made an employer liable for a hostile environment only if it knew or should have known about the harassment and failed to take prompt remedial action to end it. They reasoned that, unlike *quid pro quo* cases, in which a supervisor exerts actual authority to affect the terms, conditions, or privileges of a subordinate's employment, the supervisor is cloaked with no actual or apparent authority to create a hostile environment. In other words, the employer was directly liable for its own wrongdoing in not stopping harassment of which it was or should have been aware but was not automatically or "strictly" liable for supervisory misconduct.[82] A minority view, however, recognized vicarious liability when the harasser was a supervisor[83] and created a hostile environment through threats and intimidation.[84] Similarly, an employer without actual or constructive knowledge was generally not liable for co-worker harassment since the discriminatory conduct was not within the scope of employment and the employer usually had conferred no authority, real or apparent, to facilitate the harassment.[85] This negligence theory of employer liability continues to govern cases alleging harassment by co-workers and customers.[86]

---

[81] Meritor Savings, 477 U.S. at 70-71.

[82] See, e.g. Zimmerman v. Cook County Sheriff's Dep't, 96 F.3d 1017 (7th Cir. 1996)(employer not liable to plaintiff who complained of "personality conflict" with supervisor since absent "an Orwellian program of continuous surveillance, not yet required by law," the plaintiff must provide enough information to make a reasonable employer think there was a possibility of sexual harassment); Lipsett v. University of Puerto Rico. 864 F.2d 881, 901 (1st Cm, 1988); Bouton v. BMW of North America. inc., 29 F.3d 103 (3d Cir. 1994); Waltman v. International Paper Co., 875 F.2d 468 (5w' Cit. 1989); Juarez v. Ameritech Mobile Communications. inc., 957 F.2d 317 (701 Cit. 1992); Burns v. McGregor Elec. Indus., 995 F.2d 559 (8th Cir. 1992); Ellison v. Brady, 924 F.2d 872 (9th Cir. 1991).

[83] Kaufman v. Allied Signal, Inc., 970 F.2d 178 (6th Cir.) cert. denied, 113 S.Ct. 831 (1992).

[84] E.g. Karibian v. Columbia University, 14 F.3d 773, 780 (2d Cir. 1994) (actions of a "supervisor at a sufficiently high level in the hierarchy would necessarily be imputed to the company").

[85] See e.g. Torres v. Pisano 116 F.3d 625 (2d Cir. 1997)(university not liable for hostile environment where plaintiff complained to university official but told him to "keep it confidential."); Baker v. Weyerhauser Co.. 903 P2d 1342(10th Cir. 1990); Steele v. Offshore Shipbuilding, Inc., 867 F.2d 1311(11th Cir. 1989); Swentek v. USAir, Inc., 830 F.2d 552 (4th Cir. 1987).

[86] See, e.g., Coates v. Sundor Brands. Inc., 164 F.3d 1361 (1161 Cir. 1999)(employer not liable for co-worker harassment where plaintiff never directly discussed matter with supervisor); Lockard v. Pizza Hut, Inc.. 162 F.3d 1062 (1061 Cir. I 998)("an employer may be held

Vicarious Employer Liability and the *Ellerth/Faragher* Affirmative Defense

A different set of liability principles was adopted by the Supreme Court for supervisory harassment in *Ellerth (supra)* and *Faragher v. City of Boca Raton*.[87] While working as a lifeguard for the Parks and Recreation Department of the City of Boca Raton, *Faragher* and a female colleague were subjected to offensive touching, comments, and gestures from two supervisors. Neither lifeguard complained to department management at the time of their employment or when they resigned. In addition, lifeguards had almost no contact with City officials because they were employed at locations far removed from City Hall. However, after resigning from their positions for reasons unrelated to the alleged harassment, *Faragher* sued the City under Title VII.

Applying agency principles, the district court held the city directly liable based on the supervisory authority of the harassing employees and overall workplace structure, and indirectly liable because the harassment alleged was severe and pervasive enough to support an inference of knowledge, or constructive knowledge by the City. The Eleventh Circuit *en banc* rejected both theories and reversed. "An employer will rarely be "directly liable for hostile environment harassment," the appeals court observed, because ongoing physical and verbal harassment falls outside the scope of the supervisor's employment and is unaided by the agency relationship. Nor was the court persuaded that city officials knew, or should have known, of the harassment.

As in *Ellerth,* the *Faragher* Supreme Court largely abandoned the legal distinction between *quid pro quo* and hostile environment harassment, looking instead to agency principles as guides to employer liability for supervisory misconduct. Justice Souter's majority opinion reiterated *Ellerth's* determination that sexual harassment by a supervisor is not within the scope of employment, But because a supervisor is "aided" in his actions by the agency relationship, a more stringent vicarious liability standard was warranted than pertains to similar misconduct by mere co-workers, where the employer is liable for negligence only if he fails to abate conditions of which he "knew or should have known." "When a person with

---

liable for the harassing conduct of its customers" only on the basis of negligence, i.e. if it "fails to remedy or prevent a hostile or offensive work environment of which management-level employee's knew, or in the exercise of reasonable care should have known.").

[87] 524 U.S. 775 (1998).

circumstances. Thus, considerations of employer size and resources, and the structure of the workplace — e.g., whether a single location or on scattered sites — may be relevant factors.

Similarly, the latest High Court decisions place the burden on aggrieved employees to avail themselves of corrective procedures provided by the employer—thereby mitigating damages caused by the alleged harassment — or risk having their claim legally barred. However, whether an employee's failure to take such saving action would be deemed "unreasonable" if the complainant is able to demonstrate the inadequacy of the employer's grievance procedure, that employees had suffered retaliation for invoking the procedure in the past, or that harassing supervisors previously had not been disciplined for their action, is not addressed by the Court. Nor do the decisions specifically address the fate of employers denied the benefit of the affirmative defense because an employee followed the complaint procedure set forth in the employer's anti-harassment policy. Is strict employer liability the rule in such cases, or is the issue to be decided in light of the overall appropriateness of the employer's remedial response? Thus, many questions remain for lower courts to decide in regard to the employer's assertion of an affirmative defense. Consequently, while clarifying the law to some extent, it may take the courts years to flesh out the concept of "reasonable care," "correct promptly," "unreasonably failed," and "tangible employment action," all key elements in the Court's definition of the employer's affirmative defense.

Judicial Developments After *Ellerth* and *Faragher*

Some guidance may be gleaned from later federal appeals court decisions that have grappled with issues left unresolved by *Ellerth* and *Faragher*. Much judicial attention has focused on whether conduct alleged by the plaintiff amounts to a tangible employment action, nullifying the employer's affirmative defense, and to the adequacy of any corrective action taken by the employer in response to alleged harassment. Aside from hiring, discharge, promotion or demotion, and benefits decisions having direct economic consequences, an employment action may be "tangible" if it results in a significant change in employment status. In *Durham Life Ins. Co v. Evans*[88] a tangible employment action was found when the employer took away the plaintiff's private office and secretary, denied her of files and

---

[88] 166 F.3d 139, 153 (3d Cir. 1999).

control of funds provided by clients in order to pay premiums, and assigned her a large number of lapsed accounts. The Third Circuit reasoned, "[if an employer's act substantially decreased an employee's earning potential and caused significant disruption in his or her working conditions, a tangible adverse employment action may be found." *Reinhold v. Commonwealth of Virginia*,[89] on the other hand, found no such action where the harassing supervisor "dramatically increased" the plaintiffs workload, denied her the opportunity to attend a professional conference, and generally gave her undesirable assignments. The Fourth Circuit ruled against the plaintiff because she had not "experienced a change in her employment status akin to a demotion or a reassignment entailing significantly different job responsibilities."[90] Similarly, in *Watts v. Kroger Co.*[91] the affirmative defense was permitted to an employer who had altered the plaintiffs work schedule such that she was required to give up her second job which had previously been accommodated — one week after complaining of sexual harassment by her supervisor. According to the Fifth Circuit: "Simply changing one's work schedule is not a change in [plaintiffs] employment status. Neither is expanding the duties of one's job as a member of the produce department to include mopping the floor, cleaning the chrome in the produce department, and requiring her to check with her supervisor before taking breaks." And an employee alleging sexual harassment who ultimately quit her job could point to no "tangible" detriment where there was no showing of change in salary, benefits, duties, or prestige, but only "rude and uncivil behavior" by the employer.[92] But where a significant change of status resulted in the plaintiff being given a new, less prestigious position — amounting, in effect, to a demotion — a tangible employment action was found by another Fifth Circuit panel.[93]

The first prong of the affirmative defense requires the employer to show that it took reasonable care to prevent and promptly correct harassment. Most courts have read *Ellerth* to require, at a minimum, that the employer establish, disseminate, and enforce an anti-harassment policy and complaint procedure. Thus, in *Durham Life Ins. Co.*, the defendant was denied the *Ellerth* affirmative defense because plaintiff "was never given any literature or provided any information about the procedure to report sexual harassment

---

[89] 151 F.3d 172 (4th Cir. 1998).

[90] Id. at 175.

[91] 170 F.3d 505, 510 (5th Cir. 1999).

[92] Webb v. Cardiothoracic Surgery Associates, 139 F.3d 532 (5th Cir. 1998).

[93] Sharp v. City of Houston, 164 F.3d 923 (5th Cir. 1999) (plaintiff's transfer from prestigious Mounted Patrol to less prestigious Police Academy, although voluntary, was compelled by sexual harassment and retaliation and supported judgment against city).

and had no idea where such information could be obtained."[94] The court held that the employer's policy must be disseminated to all employees and provide an assurance that the harassing supervisor can be bypassed in registering a complaint. The defendant's complaint system in *Wilson v. Tulsa Junior College*[95] was found to be inadequate because it did not contain a provision for complaints to be filed after normal office hours. Plaintiff was a custodian and the harassment occurred during the evening shift. As a result, the employer was not entitled to the affirmative defense. And if the plaintiff's failure to invoke the employer's formal complaint procedures is not "unreasonable," the employee may still prevail, in *Sharp v. City of Houston*, the employee presented evidence that lodging a complaint was forbidden the "code of silence" which operated within the police department where she worked. Anyone using the reporting procedure would "suffer such a pattern of social ostracism and professional disapprobation that he or she would likely sacrifice a career in [the department]."[96] She also demonstrated that procedures for bypassing the harassing supervisors were ineffective. Judgment against the city was affirmed.

Beyond adopting an anti-harassment policy and procedures for its employees, the employer must undertake immediate and appropriate corrective action — including discipline proportionate to the seriousness of the offense — when it learns of a violation.[97] Whether the employer has responded in a prompt and reasonable manner depends on all the underlying facts and circumstances, and the harassment victim's own conduct may be a relevant factor. Thus, in *Coates v. Sundor Brands, Inc.*[98] the Eleventh Circuit found that the employer's reaction to a complaint was adequate, even though delayed for a period of twenty months, because the employee's initial allegations were not sufficiently specific to warrant an earlier response by the employer. The plaintiff originally requested that no work assignment be changed, forcing her continued regular contact with the harasser, and repeatedly assured the human resources manager that the circumstances were fine. The employer took immediate action to suspend the harasser when the

---

[94] Supra n. 87, at p. 162.

[95] 164 F.3d 534 (10th Cir. 1998).

[96] 164 F.3d at 931-32.

[97] See Skidmore v. Precision Printing and Packaging, Inc., 188 F.3d 606 (5th Cir. 1999) (employer not liable because it took "prompt remedial action" when it instructed alleged harasser to leave plaintiff alone and moved her to a new shift even though no investigation was conducted until complaint was filed with EEOC six months later); Mockler v. Multnomah County, 140 F.3d 808 813 (9th Cir. 1998).

[98] 164 F.3d 1361 (11th Cir. 1999).

plaintiff was finally candid about her problems.[99] In some cases, alleged harassers who were discharged but later exonerated have sued their employers. The employer has usually prevailed, however, as long as the decision to fire or otherwise discipline the suspected perpetrator was based on a good faith belief of misconduct after an adequate investigation was performed. "The real issue is whether the employer reasonably believed the employee's allegation [of harassment] and acted on it in good faith, or to the contrary. the employer did not actually believe the co-employee's allegation but instead used it as a pretext for an otherwise discriminatory dismissal."[100]

Even before the High Court's latest decisions, lower court rulings suggested that the most effective defensive strategy for employers to avoid liability for a hostile work environment was a proactive approach. Thus, in *McKenzie v. Illinois Department of Transportation*,[101] the "prompt and remedial action" taken by the state employer in barring further workplace contacts between the allegedly harassing co-worker and the complainant was held to prevent recovery on a hostile environment claim. In addition, the courts have generally been reluctant to impose Title VII liability on employers who act "prophylactically" to stem harassing conditions before they begin. This is illustrated by *Gary v. Long*[102] where the D.C. Circuit dismissed a hostile environment lawsuit against the Washington Metropolitan Area Transit Authority (WMATA) as the result of repeated verbal and physical harassment, and eventual rape, of a female employee by a supervisor. Claims of quid pro quo harassment were rejected due to lack of economic detriment. Moreover, WMATA escaped liability on the hostile environment claim because it had an "active and firm" policy against the sexual harassment, which it publicized through staff notices, seminars, and

---

[99] See also Indest v. Freeman Decorating, inc., 164 F.3d 258 (5th Cir. l999)(employer not liable for a vice president's sexual harassment when it took prompt and effective action upon learning of the situation); Van Zant v. KLM Royal Dutch Airlines. 80 F. 3d 708, 715 (2d Cir. 1996)(employer's response prompt where it began investigation on the day that complaint was made, conducted interviews within two days. and fired harasser within ten days); Steiner v. Showboat Operating Co.. 25 F.3d 1459 (9th Cir. 1994), cert. denied, 513 U.S. 1082 (1995)(employer's response to complaints inadequate despite eventual discharge of harasser where it did not seriously investigate or strongly reprimand supervisor until after plaintiff filed charge with state FEP agency).

[100] Waggoner v. City of Garland Tex., 987 F.2d 1160, 1165 (5th Cir. 1993). See also Cotran v. Rollins Hudig Hall International, Inc., 17 Cal. 45th 93 (1998); Morrow v. Wal-Mart Stores, Inc., 152 F.3d 559 (7th Cir. 1998).

[101] 92 F.3d 4743 (7th Cir. 1996).

[102] 59 F.3d 1391 (D.C. Cir 1995). See also, Farley v. American Cast Iron Pipe Company, 115 F.3d 1548 (11th Cir. 1997).

EEO counselors, and because it maintained detailed grievance procedures for reporting acts of discrimination.

The practical lesson for employers is to formulate and communicate to employees a specific policy forbidding workplace harassment; to establish procedures for reporting incidents of harassment that bypass the immediate supervisor of the victim if he or she is the alleged harasser; to immediately investigate all alleged incidents and order prompt corrective action (including make-whole relief for the victim) when warranted; and to appropriately discipline the harasser.

Personal Liability of Harassing Supervisors and Co-workers

Some division of judicial opinion persists, again because "agent[s]" are included within the Title VII definition of "employer," as to the personal liability of individual supervisors and co-workers for hostile environment harassment or other discriminatory conduct. A majority of federal circuit courts to address the question—the Second,[103] Fifth,[104] Seventh,[105] Ninth,[106] Tenth[107] and Eleventh[108] and District of Columbia[109]—have interpreted agents in the statutory definition as merely incorporating *respondeat superior* and refused to impose personal liability on agents. These courts also note the incongruity of imposing personal liability on individuals while capping compensatory and punitive damages based on employer size, as the statute does, and exempting small businesses that employ less than 15 persons from Title VII altogether, Of the Courts of Appeals, only the Fourth Circuit[110] has extended Title VII liability to supervisors in both their personal capacity where the supervisor exercised significant control over the plaintiff's hiring, firing, or conditions of employment. The First Circuit, the Third Circuit, the Sixth Circuit, and the Eight Circuit have yet to decide the issue, leading to contradictory results among the district courts in those jurisdictions.[111]

---

[103] Tomka v. Seiler Corp. 66 F.3d 1295 (2d Cir. 1995).

[104] Grant v. Loan Star Co., 21 F.3d 649 (5th Cir.), cert. denied, 115 S. Ct. 574 (1994).

[105] EEOC v. AIC Sec. Investigations, Ltd., 55 F.3d 1276 (7th Cir. 1995).

[106] Miller v. Maxwell's Int'l Inc., 991 F.2d 583 (9th Cir. 1993), cert, denied, 114 S. Ct. 1049 (1994).

[107] Haynes v. Williams, 88 F.3d 989 (10th Cir. 1996).

[108] Busby v. City of Orlando, 931 F.2d 764 (11th Cir. 1991).

[109] Gary v. Long, 59 F.3d 1391 (D.C. Cir. 1995), cert. denied, 116 S.Ct. 569 (1995).

[110] See Paroline v. Unisys Corp., 879 F.2d 100 (4th Cir. 1989), rev'd in part, aff'd in relevant part, 9090 F.2d 27 (4th Cir. 1990) (en blanc).

[111] See Hernandez v. Wangen, 938 F. Supp. 1052 (D.P.R. 1996) and cases listed therein.

SEXUAL HARASSMENT IN THE SCHOOLS

Issues surrounding the legal responsibility of school districts or other educational authorities for sexual harassment within the schools are highlighted by recent media reports of harassment of students by teachers and of disciplinary proceedings against students for alleged sexual abuse or unwanted displays of affection directed at their peers. Title IX of the 1972 Education Amendments provides that "[no] person in the United States shall, on the basis of sex, be excluded from participation in, be denied the benefits of, or be subjected to discrimination under any education program or activity receiving Federal financial assistance"[112] Under the statute, student victims of any form of sex discrimination, including sexual harassment, may file a written complaint with the Office of Civil Rights (OCR)[113] for administrative determination and possible imposition of sanctions—including termination of federal funding—upon the offending educational institution. In addition, school personnel who harass students may be sued individually for monetary damages and other civil remedies under 42 U.S.C. § 1983 prohibiting the deprivation of federally protected rights under "color of law."

Title IX also provides student victims with an avenue of judicial relief In *Cannon v. University of Chicago*,[114] the Supreme Court ruled that an implied right of action exists under Title IX for student victims of sex discrimination who need not exhaust their administrative remedies before filing suit. However, the availability of monetary damages under Title IX remained uncertain until *Franklin v. Gwinnett County Public Schools*.[115] In Franklin, a female high school student brought an action for damages under Title IX against her school district alleging that she had been subjected to sexual harassment and abuse by a teacher. The Supreme Court held that damages were available to the sexual harassment victim if she could prove that the school district had intentionally violated Title IX. After Franklin, Title TX had been held to prohibit both *quid pro quo* and hostile environment teacher-student harassment. There was less judicial consensus, however, regarding legal standards for holding an educational institution liable for a sexually hostile educational environment created by student or teacher misconduct.

The appropriate standard for measuring a school district's liability for sexual abuse of a student by a teacher remained unsettled until the Supreme

---

[112] 20 U.S.C. Sec. 1681(a).
[113] 34 C.F.R. Sec. 100.7(d)(1)(1995).
[114] 441 U.S. 677 (1979).
[115] 503 U.S.. 60 (1992).

Court ruling in *Gebser v. Lago Vista Independent School District*.[116] The federal courts of appeals and district courts had adopted a variety of standards, including strict liability;[117] a "knew or should have known" negligence standard;[118] a theory of intentional discrimination;[119] or imputed liability based on principles of agency law.[120] In a series of three rulings, the Fifth Circuit has rejected each of these approaches in favor of a more stringent standard requiring "actual knowledge" by responsible school officials.[121]

On June 22, 1998, in *Gebser*, the Supreme Court answered the question of what standard of liability to apply to school districts under Title IX where a teacher harasses a student without the knowledge of school administrators. Jane Doe, a thirteen-year-old student, had been sexually abused by a teacher, but there was no evidence that any school official was aware of the situation until after it ended. Instead of strict liability or theory of constructive notice, Doe relied on the familiar common law principle later applied by the Court in *Ellerth* and *Faragher* that an employer is vicariously liable for an employee's injurious actions, even if committed outside the scope of employment, if the employee "was aided in accomplishing the tort by the existence of the agency relationship"[122] According to this theory. the harasser's status as a reacher made his abuse possible by placing him in an authoritative position to take advantage of his adolescent student. Because teachers are almost always "aided" by the agency relationship, however, and application of the common law rule "would generate vicarious liability in virtually every case of teacher-student harassment." The Fifth Circuit rejected the approach in favor of its actual knowledge standard.

In a 5 to 4 opinion by Justice O'Connor, the Supreme Court affirmed, avoided any comparison to the strict liability and affirmative defense

[116] 118 S.Ct. 1989 (1998).

[117] See Bolon v. Rolla Public School, 917 F. Supp. 1423 (E.D. Mo. 1996).

[118] Deborah O. v. Lake Central School Corp. 61 F.3d 9095 (7th Cir. 1995)(school liable if it "knew or should have known about the harassment and yet failed to take appropriate remedial action").

[119] RLR v. Prague Public School District I-103, 838 F.Supp. 1526 (W.D. Okla. 1993) (school district not liable for sexual abuse by basketball coach because parents of student victim "failed to come forward with any facts showing the custom or policy, acquiescence in, conscious disregard of, or failure to investigate or discipline on the part of the school district").

[120] Doe v. Claiborne County, Tennessee, 103 F.3d 495 (6th Cir. 1996) (institution not liable unless teacher is aided in the harassment by an agency relationship with the institution).

[121] Canutillo Independent School District v. Leija, 101 F3d 393 (5th Cir. 1996); Rosa H. v. San Elizario Independent School District, 106 F.3d 648 (5th Cir. 1997); Doe v. Lago Vista Independent School District, 106 F.3d 1223 (5th Cir. 1997).

[122] Id. at 1225 (citing Restatement (Second) of Agency Sec. 219(2)(d)(1958).

framework promulgated for Title VII employment law. It held that a student who has been sexually harassed by a teacher may not recover damages against the school district "unless an official of the school district who at a minimum has authority to institute corrective measures on the district's behalf has actual knowledge of; and is deliberately indifferent to, the teacher's misconduct." The differing legislative constructs of Title VII and Title IX, and an apparent reluctance to impose excessive financial liability on schools, appeared to drive the Court's decision.

Unlike Title VII, Title IX has been judicially determined to provide only an "implied" private right of action and rather than a statute of general application, it imposes legal obligations only as a condition to the receipt of federal financial assistance. These distinctions persuaded the Court to "shape a sensible remedial scheme that best comports with the statute" and its legislative history. In analyzing congressional intent, the Court examined the statutory provisions for Title IX enforcement by means of federal agency termination of federal funds to non-complying school districts following notice and opportunity to be heard. Given the express notice requirement of the statute, the majority felt it unfair to impose a vicarious or constructive notice standard on school districts in private lawsuits. Moreover, there was concern that the award of damages in any given case might unfairly exceed the amount of federal funding actually received by the school. Consequently, there was no actionable Title IX claim since responsible school administrators were without notice or "actual knowledge" of the alleged sexual relationship. The Court summarily noted that Lago Vista's failure to promulgate and publicize an anti-harassment policy and grievance procedure, as mandated by U. S. Department of Education regulations, established neither actual notice, deliberate indifference, or even discrimination under Title IX.

The dissenters argued that the rationale for Title VII *respondeat superior* or vicarious liability — to induce the employer to take corrective action and limit damages — also applied to Title IX sexual harassment. Justice Stevens contended that the majority's rule creates the opposite incentive, encouraging schools to insulate themselves from knowledge, and predicted that few Title IX plaintiffs who have been sexually harassed will be able to recover damages under "this exceedingly high standard." in addition to urging vicarious liability, Justice Ginsburg proposed to permit schools, akin to the standard in *Faragher*, to assert internal procedures as an affirmative defense.

Davis v. Monroe County Board of Education, decided in 1999. addressed the standard of liability that should be imposed on school districts to remedy student-on-student harassment.[123] The plaintiff in Davis alleged that her fifth-grade daughter had been harassed by another student over a prolonged period — a fact reported to teachers on several occasions -- but that school officials had failed to take corrective action. Justice O'Connor, writing for a sharply divided court, determined that the plaintiff had stated a Title IX claim. Because the statute restricts the actions of federal grant recipients, however, and not the conduct of third parties, the Court again refused to impose vicarious liability on the school district. Instead, "a recipient of federal funds may be liable in damages tinder Title IX only for its own misconduct." School authorities' own "deliberate indifference" to student-on-student harassment could violate Title TX in certain cases. Thus, the Court held, where officials have "actual knowledge" of the harassment, where the "harasser is under the school's disciplinary authority," and where the harassment is so severe "that it can be said to deprive the victims of access to the educational opportunities or benefits provided by the school," the district may be held liable for damages under Title IX.

In qualifying the *Davis* standard, the Court suggests that student harassment may be far more difficult to prove than sexual harassment in employment. Beyond requiring "actual knowledge," Justice O'Connor cautioned that "schools are unlike adult workplaces" and disciplinary decisions of school administrators are not to be "second guess[ed]" by lower courts unless "clearly unreasonable" under the circumstances. Additionally, the majority emphasized that "damages are not available for simple acts of teasing and name-calling among school children, even where these comment target differences in gender." In effect, *Davis* left to school administrators the task of drawing the line between innocent teasing and actionable sexual harassment — a difficult and legally perilous task at best.

On March 13, 1997, before the Supreme Court ruling in *Gebser,* OCR issued a policy guidance addressing the institutional liability of school

---

[123] Prior to Davis. the federal appeals Courts were divided between those which refused to award Title TX damages or injunctive relief against a school district for student-on-student or "peer" sexual harassment, Rowinsky v. Bryan Independent School District, 80 F.3d 1006 (5th Cir.), cert. denied 519 U.S. 861 (1996), Davis v. Monroe. 120 F.3d 1390 (11th Cir. 1997) and others, which had applied agency principles and Title VII legal standards to hold school officials liable for failure to take reasonable steps to prevent known hostile environment harassment by students or other third parties. Murray v. New York Univ. College of Dentistry, 57 F.3d 243. 248-50 (2d Cir. 1995)(discussing Title VII standards in analyzing Title IX sexual harassment claim); Brown v. Hot. Sexy and Safer Products, Inc., 68 F.3d 525. 540 (1st Cir. 1995)(applying Title VII principles to Title IX hostile environment sexual harassment claim). cert. denied 516 U.S. 1159 (1996) and Clyde K. v. Puyallup School Dist., 35 F.3d 1396, 1402 (9th Cir. 1994)("school officials might reasonably be concerned about liability for failing to remedy peer sexual harassment that exposes female students to a hostile educational environment.

districts for harassment of students by teachers or other students. That policy states that a school district or other funded educational agency may be liable under Title IX if the institution knew, or should have known, that a student was being subjected to hostile environment sexual harassment by other students and fails to take appropriate corrective action. For *quid pro quo* harassment of a student by a teacher or other employee—involving, for example, use of grading authority to extort sexual favors—a district "will always be liable for even one instance" of abuse, regardless of its actual or constructive knowledge. Liability for a "hostile or abusive educational environment" attaches, according to OCR, if the harassing teacher or employee "reasonably" appeared to act on the school's behalf, i.e. with "apparent authority" or was "aided" in the harassment by reason of "position of authority" with the institution. A school district is also liable under the guidance if it fails to take immediate and appropriate steps to remedy known harassment.[124] These standards appear to conflict with *Gebser* and *Davis* insofar as they would permit finding an institution liable for student harassment based on "constructive knowledge"— that is, what school administrators reasonably should have known — or the "apparent authority" of the alleged harasser, regardless of what they actually knew.

VIOLENCE AGAINST WOMEN ACT

The Violence Against Women Act (VAWA) was enacted by Congress in 1994 "to protect the civil rights of victims of gender-motivated violence." It imposed new criminal penalties for certain specified offences and created a private cause of action for civil damages against persons who perpetrate "crime[s] of violence motivated by gender."[125] Specific "crimes of violence" triggering statutory coverage include "State or Federal offenses" that would constitute "a felony against the person. . .or a felony against the property," as recognized by federal law,[126] and which pose "a serious risk of physical injury to another," whether or not the misconduct alleged ever resulted in actual charges or a prior criminal action. To be actionable under VAWA, however, the complainant has to show that the offense was "motivated by gender," i.e., that the predicate crime was committed "because of gender or

---

[124] Sexual Harassment of Students by School Employees, Other Students, or Third Parties, 62 Fed. Reg. 12034, 12039-40 (1997).

[125] 42 U.S.C. Sec. 13981.

[126] 18 U.S.C. Sec. 16. In effect, the bill incorporates the existing federal criminal code definition of "crime of violence" as predicate for a civil rights violation under VAWA.

on the basis of gender,"[127] and was at least partially due to "an animus based on the victim's gender."

According to the legislative history, "proof of 'gender motivation' under Title III," of VAWA is to "proceed in the same ways proof of race or sex discrimination proceeds under other civil rights laws. Judges and juries will determine 'motivation' from the 'totality of the circumstances' surrounding the event."[128] In this regard, legal standards for proof of "hate crimes" may be "useful," such as "language used by the perpetrator; the severity of the attack (including mutilation); the lack of provocation; previous history of similar incidents; absence of any other apparent motive (battery without robbery, for example); common sense."[129] In other words, no cause of action will lie for injury resulting from mere "random" acts of violence, regardless of the gender of the victim, where it is not proven that the perpetrator was gender-motivated.[130]

The enforcement mechanism provided for this new right to be free of gender-motivated violent crime is a private civil action in federal (or state) court. The prevailing plaintiff in a judicial action may obtain compensatory and punitive damages, injunctive relief and "such other relief as the court deems appropriate." While predicated upon conduct that is made criminal by other federal and state law provisions, the statute does not require a prior criminal complaint, prosecution, or conviction to establish the elements of a cause of action. No federal administrative scheme is authorized for VAWA enforcement.[131] But parallel civil and criminal proceedings for conduct, which constitutes a VAWA offense, are not precluded.

To some extent, VAWA overlapped and supplemented the protection of Title VII for women victimized by gender-motivated violence and harassment in the workplace. Title VII applies only to employment, but even there excludes a large segment of the national workforce employed by companies and firms with fewer than 15 employees. A condition precedent to a Title VII judicial action is that the complaining employee or applicant first resort to the EEOC administrative process for voluntary negotiation and conciliation of the matter between the parties. Moreover, while the 1991

---

[127] Id. at Sec. 13981(e)(1).

[128] S. Rep. No. 103-138, at 52 (1992).

[129] Id. at 52 n. 61.

[130] Under evidentiary standards prescribed by Sec. 13981(e)(1), the complainant must prove gender motivation "by a preponderance of the evidence."

[131] This is in contrast to the voluntary negotiation and conciliation procedures of the Equal Employment Commission, which must be pursued before filing a federal lawsuit seeking relief from sexual harassment in the workplace under Title VII of the 1964 Civil Rights Act. 42 U.S.C. Sections 2000e et seq.

amendments added provisions for jury trials and compensatory and punitive damage awards in Title VI actions, such relief is limited by monetary "caps" that find no parallel in later law. The element of "violence," however, is not a requisite of the offense under either the Title VII or Title IX.

The 1994 law's statement of purpose anchored the civil rights remedy for gender-motivated violence to the "affirmative" power of Congress under the Commerce Clause of the U.S. Constitution and § 5 of the Fourteenth Amendment. Congressional power to prohibit or remedy equal protection or due process violations has historically been limited by judicial construction of the Fourteenth Amendment to "state action" or private conduct actively supported by the state or its agents. As discussed below. The power of Congress to regulate purely private conduct pursuant to its §5 power, always problematic, may now be a dead letter Similarly, recent Supreme Court rulings have largely eviscerated congressional authority to regulate non-economic activities "affecting commerce" by application of civil or criminal sanctions.

In United States v. Lopez,[132] the Supreme Court invalidated, as exceeding Congress' commerce powers, the Gun-Free School Zones Act of 1990[133], which made a federal offense of possessing a firearm within 1.000 feet of a school. As traditionally applied, the Commerce Clause permits Congress to regulate "use of the channels" and "instrumentalities" of interstate commerce, as well as activities within a state that "substantially affect" its flow. Despite the absence of congressional findings, the Government in Lopez claimed that the statute regulated an activity, which substantially impacted interstate commerce because possession of firearms in a school zone may result in an increase in violent crime. Criminal violence, in turn, affects the national economy 'by increasing insurance costs, reducing the willingness of persons to travel to areas of the country perceived as unsafe, and by diminishing productivity due to impaired student learning environments. The Supreme Court concluded, however, that the regulated activity—firearm possession within a school zone—was beyond Congress' constitutional reach since it had "nothing to do with 'commerce' or any sort of economic enterprise, however broadly one might define those terms." The Court rejected the Government's "cost of crime" argument as an overly expansive theory, which would permit Congress to "regulate not only all violent crime, but all activities that might lead to violent crime, regardless of how tenuously they relate to interstate commerce." Were this argument successful, the Court reasoned, "it is difficult to perceive any limitation on

---

[132] 514 U.S. 549 (1995).

federal power, even in areas such as criminal law enforcement or education where States historically have been sovereign."

The first criminal prosecution under VAWA involved a husband who was convicted of interstate domestic violence for severely beating his wife in their home and subsequently driving her in and out of West Virginia for a period of five days before taking her to a hospital in Kentucky. On appeal, in United States v. Bailey,[134] the defendant challenged his conviction on the grounds that the interstate domestic violence statute, 18 U.S.C. § 2261(a), exceeded Congress' powers under Lopez since it concerned neither "channels" nor "instrumentalities" of commerce, and was not related in any "substantial" way to commercial activity. The Fourth Circuit disagreed, upholding both the VAWA provision and the conviction. Lopez was distinguished as not applicable to the domestic violence statute, which required the crossing of a state line, "thus placing the transaction squarely in interstate commerce." Constitutional support for VAWA was drawn from earlier decisions approving the White Slave Traffic Act of 1910[135] and the Mann Act[136], which condemned transportation in interstate commerce for various "immoral" purposes. In other words, the Lopez analysis was not relevant to the VAWA criminal provision, which incorporates an interstate component similar to these earlier statutes and "requires the commission of a crime of violence causing bodily injury, which certainly is not different from the immoral purpose forbade in Cleveland and the debauchery forbade in Caminetti."

Likewise, the Eighth Circuit U.S. Court of Appeals in United States v. Wright[137] sustained a VAWA provision making it a federal crime to cross a state line with the intent to violate a state protective order and then to violate it.[138] A federal district court had voided the statute on the grounds that crossing state lines to violate a protective order was not a commercial activity and "does not substantially affect interstate commerce." The appeals court agreed that the "affecting commerce" test of Lopez was not germane but rejected the conclusion that crossing state lines for noncommercial purposes is not interstate commerce, Judicial rulings upholding a variety of federal offenses, from Mann Act to the crime of traveling in interstate commerce to avoid prosecution, had consistently affirmed that "crossing state lines, without more, is interstate commerce." Also relevant was the fact

---

[133] 18 U.S.C. Sec. 922(a)(1)(A).
[134] 112 F.3d 758 (4th Cir. 1997).
[135] Caminetti v. United States, 242 U.S. 470 (1917).
[136] Cleveland v. United States, 329 U.S. 14 (1946).
[137] 128 F.3d 1274 (1997).
[138] 18 U.S.C. Sec. 2262(a)(1).

that the statute required not only the crossing of a state line with prohibited intent, hut that the perpetrator actually act on that intent, The defendant's Tenth Amendment challenge to the statute was also rejected.

Early judicial challenges to VAWA's civil remedy provision had also affirmed a relatively expansive interpretation of congressional power. In Doe v. Doe.[139] the plaintiff alleged a pattern of "systematic and continuous" physical and emotional abuse at the hands of her spouse over a seventeen year period resulting in severe emotional distress, trauma, and depression. The defendant spouse moved to dismiss, claiming that Congress lacked authority under either the Commerce Clause or the Fourteenth Amendment to enact the VAWA remedy for gender-based violence. The federal district court rejected the motion, however, finding support for Congress' judgment that violence against women was a "national problem with substantial impact on interstate commerce." A "rational basis" for the legislation was found in "statistical, medical, and economic data before the Congress" that was lacking in Lopez. The Senate Report, for example, indicated that 50% of rape victims leave the work force involuntarily and that "fear of gender-based crimes restricts movement, reduces employment opportunities, increases health expenditures, and reduces consumer spending, all of which affect interstate commerce and the national economy.[140] Moreover, VAWA was found to "complement" rather than encroach upon state procedures because it remedied "deficiencies" in existing state and federal legal protections against gender-based violence while preserving traditional state tort remedies. The federal safeguards were further justified, said the Doe Court, given the special harm, community unrest, and likelihood of retaliation, provoked by bias-inspired crime.

The constitutionality of VAWA's civil damages remedy for gender-based violence[141] had been sustained by eleven federal district courts when the Fourth Circuit en banc reversed an earlier panel decision and invalidated the statute.[142] In U.S. v. Morrison,[143] the Supreme Court affirmed the appeals court's conclusion that the civil remedy provision of VAWA exceeded Congress' constitutional authority. The case involved a civil action by a female Virginia Tech student against two male student athletes who verbally berated and raped her three times within minutes of their first meeting. Administrative proceedings against the perpetrators under the university's

---

[139] 929 F.Supp. 608 (D.Conn. 1996).

[140] S. Rep. 138, 103d Cong., 1st Sess. 54 (1993).

[141] 42 U.S.C. Sec. 13981(c).

[142] Brzonkala v. Virginia Polytechnic and State

[143] 120 S. Ct. 1740 (2000).

"Sexual Assault Policy" were dismissed or set-aside on two separate occasions, and the sexual violence had gone unpunished by state officials, when the female victim turned for relief to the federal courts. The district judge was convinced by the "totality of circumstances" — including vulgar statements made by the defendants concerning the assaults and the "gang rape" aspect of the ease that "gender animus" was the underlying motivation for the crime. But he voided the statute, since to equate the impact of gender-motivated crime with interstate commerce would "extend Congress' power . . . and unreasonably tip the balance away from the states."

That decision was reviewed initially by a three-judge appellate panel, which applied a "rational basis" standard in concluding that the "regulated activity" substantially affected interstate commerce. In contrast to the congressional silence in *Lopez*, the *Brzonkala* panel cited "voluminous findings" from the committee reports on the social and economic costs of gender-motivated crimes which warranted judicial deference and a "strong presumption of validity and constitutionality" In a an *en banc* rehearing, the full Fourth Circuit reversed, finding it "impossible to link such violence with a particular interstate market or with any specific obstruction of interstate commerce." Rather, the relationship between gender violence and commerce was too "attenuated" and indistinguishable from that existing "between any significant activity and interstate commerce." Invoking federalism concerns, the court declined to "rely[ ] on arguments that lack any principled limitations and [that] would, if accepted, convert the power to regulate interstate commerce into a general police power."

These proceedings set the stage for the Supreme Court's long awaited decision on May 16, 2000 in *U.S. v. Morrison*, holding that Congress had overstepped its constitutional hounds when it passed the VAWA civil remedy. Declaring that "the Constitution requires a distinction between what is truly national and which is truly local," a five-Justice majority led by the Chief Justice rejected each of the two sources of constitutional authority asserted by Congress to support the legislation. The law was neither a valid regulation of interstate commerce nor a proper means of enforcing the equal protection guarantee of the Fourteenth Amendment. The commerce clause provided no basis for the Act, the Court said, despite the extensive record compiled and the findings enacted that the problem of violence against women had a substantial and deleterious effect on commerce. Just as the "non-economic, criminal nature of the conduct at issue" was crucial to the demise of the Gun-Free School Zone Act in Lopez, gender-motivated crimes of violence were, for the majority, "not in any sense of the phrase economic activity." Thus, congressional findings to the effect that gender-based violence deterred travel or employment of victims, diminished national productivity or added to national medical costs did not rationally support the legislation or require deference by the Court. In addition, the findings were "substantially weakened" by a "but-for causal chain," allowing "Congress to regulate any crime as long as the nationwide, aggregated impact of that crime has substantial effects on employment, production, transit, or consumption." Such reasoning was faulty under Lopez, the majority argued, because it would permit federal regulation of family law and other traditional areas of state concern, "completely obliterat[ing] the Constitution's distinction between national and local authority."

Section 5 of the Fourteenth Amendment likewise provided no basis for the civil remedy provision because the constitutional guarantee of equal protection is directed at the states and its officials, not at private "individuals who have committed criminal acts motivated by gender bias," who are the sole targets of the statute. Since the VAWA civil remedy did nothing to the states or state officers, it was not a valid exercise of the § 5 enforcement power. The Court also noted that the statute applies uniformly throughout the states, while the legislative record failed to demonstrate that gender-motivated crimes occur equally in all states, or even most states. Therefore, the VAWA remedy did not meet the judicial requirements of "congruence" and proportionality" with the problem it seeks to address. The Court did not explain why Congress could not, if it decided the states were failing because of prejudice or animus to protect women, provide a federal remedy against private individuals.

Joining Chief Justice Rehnquist in the majority were Justices O'Connor, Scalia, Kennedy, and Thomas. Justice Souter dissented, along with Justices Stevens, Ginsburg, and Breyer, who charged that the majority with revision of the substantial effects test under the commerce clause by discounting its "cumulative effects and rational basis features." This "defect" in the majority's reasoning was its "rejection of the Founders' considered judgment that politics, not judicial review, should mediate between state and national interests as the strength and legislative jurisdiction of the National Government inevitably increased through the expected growth of the national economy."

UNITED STATES V. LANIER

On March 31, 1997, the U.S. Supreme Court vacated a ruling by the Sixth Circuit U.S. Court of Appeals which had reversed the conviction of

David Lanier, a Tennessee Chancery Court judge, for willful deprivation of federal constitutional "rights, privileges, or immunities" under color of law in violation of 18 U.S.C. Sec. 242. The charges against Lanier stem from allegations that he raped. assaulted, or harassed eight women in his chambers who either worked for the judge, worked with him, or had cases pending before his court. The "right, privilege or immunity" allegedly violated was identified as a Fourteenth Amendment due process guarantee of "bodily integrity"—specifically, the right to be free of sexual assault by a state official. After a trial, Lanier was convicted on two felony and five misdemeanor counts of violating Sec. 242 and was sentenced to a total of twenty-five years in prison. A panel of the Court of Appeals for the Sixth Circuit affirmed the conviction and sentence, but the full court overturned the decision and granted rehearing *en banc*.[144]

Invoking established rules of construction for criminal statutes, and the Supreme Court ruling in *Screws v. United States*,[145] the en banc majority set-aside the conviction on the grounds that existing § 242 precedents failed to adequately notify the public that simple or sexual assault crimes invaded a constitutional right or liberty protected by the statute. To avoid unconstitutional vagueness, a plurality of the Screws Court had construed the statute to require proof of "specific intent" to deprive the victim of a right "made specific either by the express terms of the Constitution...or by decisions interpreting them." The Federal Government had argued that a due process right to be free of unwarranted assault recognized by lower court decisions in other contexts provided adequate notice of criminal conduct to be punished. But due to the statute's "abstract" nature, and discrepancies among the circuits and federal district courts in their recognition of "new" constitutional rights, Chief Judge Merritt felt that "[o]nly a Supreme Court decision with nationwide application can make specific a right that can result in § 242 liability" and only when the right had been made to apply in "a factual situation fundamentally similar to the one at bar." The en banc court conceded the "outrageous" nature of Judge Lanier' s conduct, but found that since the Supreme Court had not so ruled in a "fundamentally similar" situation, the supposed right to be free of sexual assault could not form the basis for a federal prosecution.

Writing for a unanimous Supreme Court, Justice Souter faulted the Sixth Circuit for applying too restrictive a standard and for concluding that §242 could never incorporate "newly-created constitutional rights." The "fair warning" requirement in *Screws* was not a "categorical rule" excluding from

---

[144] 43 F.3d 1033 (6th Cir. 1995).

the universe of §242 safeguards any right not specifically identified by prior Supreme Court decisional law. To interpret the statute so restrictively, said the Court, was "unsound," contradicting both the legislative and judicial history of the criminal civil rights provisions and decisional law governing the corollary "clearly established" qualified immunity standard applied by the courts to determine civil liability of state officials under 42 U.S.C. 1983. The "touchstone" for imposing § 242 criminal liability is whether the statute, either standing alone or as construed by the courts at all levels, "made it reasonably clear at the relevant time that the defendant's conduct was criminal." According to Justice Souter, general statements of the law" could provide "fair and clear wanting" and may apply "with obvious clarity," in at least some situations, even though the particular conduct in question had not previously been held unlawful in precisely the same circumstances.

The Supreme Court's disposition of *Lanier* avoided decision of the main substantive issue in the case—that is, the constitutional status of the right to be free from sexual harassment and abuse at the hands of state officials. Other aspects of the ruling, however, and its contemporary legal background suggested the probable legal outcome of the case on remand. First, in a concluding footnote the Court rejected "as plainly without merit" several arguments—including the unavailability of § 242 to enforce due process rights—made by Judge Lanier and relied upon by the Sixth Circuit to reach its earlier decision. This complicated the task of defending Judge Lanier's position on remand. In his background discussion of the case, Justice Souter also quotes with seeming approval from the trial judge's instruction to the jury that the Fourteenth Amendment protection of bodily integrity includes "the right to be free from certain sexually motivated physical assaults and coerced sexual battery." This instruction appears to conform to the weight of existing lower federal court precedent, including a Sixth Circuit decision since *Lanier*,[146] making it difficult for the appeals court to reiterate its earlier finding that Judge Lanier did not have "fair warning" that his conduct violated constitutional rights.[147] In addition, Congress has enacted legislation

---

[145] 325 U.S. 91 (1945).

[146] Doe v. Claiborne County, 103 F.3d 495 (6th Cir. 1996).

[147] See, e.g., Doe v. Taylor Independent School District, 15 F.3d 443, 451 (5th Cir.), cert. denied, 115 S. Ct. 70 (1994) (teacher's sexual abuse of a student "deprived [the student] of a liberty interest recognized under the substantive due process component of the Fourteenth Amendment"); Dan Vang v. Vang Xiong X. Toyed, 944 F.2d 476, 479 (9th Cir. 1991)(plaintiff's constitutional right were violated in a § 1983 case when she was raped by a state welfare official); and Stoneking v. Bradford Area School District, 882 F.2d 720, 727 (3d Cir. 1989), cert. denied, 493 U.S. 1044 (1990) ("the constitutional right ... to freedom from invasion of ... personal security through sexual abuse, was well established" by the early 1980's).

based on the assumption that § 242 punishes sexual assaults.[148] Finally, the US Justice Department brief in Lanier noted that it prosecutes thirty cases per year under § 242, many based on a due process right to bodily integrity. Since 1981, the Civil Rights Division of DOJ had prosecuted at least twenty-nine §242 cases involving sexual assault by public officials) most involving a woman who was sexually assaulted by a jailor, police officer, or border patrol agent. However, three other cases besides *Lanier* involved sexual assault by state judges—two resulting in guilty pleas, the third in acquittal.

In sum, *Lanier* questioned the fundamental nature of "constitutional crimes" prohibited by § 242, a statute notable for its definitional vagueness and described by the court of appeals as "perhaps the most abstractly worded statute among the more than 700 crimes in the federal criminal code." Since the federal "rights, privileges, or immunities" whose official invasion may be the predicate for a § 242 prosecution are not plainly spelled out by statute, its scope has traditionally been determined by the courts according to contemporary constitutional understanding of those terms. Justice Souter, in his opinion, appears largely unmoved by respondent's argument that to permit a § 242 prosecution of Judge Lanier would encroach upon the traditional police powers of the state and impermissibly "federalize," by judicial decree, state offenses like rape and sexual assault into a federal "common law" of crime. Nonetheless, as noted earlier, solicitude for federalism and our dual system of government was a factor limiting Congress' commerce power to enact the Gun-Free School Zones Act in Lopez and could inform judicial review of the corollary issue posed by Lanier To what extent, if any, such objections may influence renewed judicial consideration of the case can only be speculated. At this point, however, Lanier appears to expand the general availability of § 242 as a safeguard against official deprivation of federal constitutional rights and, in addition, may constitutionally buttress the civil remedy for gender-motivated violence in VAWA, at least as applied to acts of violence by governmental agents or others acting under color of law.

---

[148] In the Violent Crime Control and Law Enforcement Act of 1994, Congress required enhanced punishment for several crimes in aggravated circumstances, including sexual violence. That enhancement provision applied to violations of § 242. See P.L. 103-322 § 320103(b)(3), 108 Stat. 2109.

Chapter 4

VIOLENCE AGAINST WOMEN ACT: HISTORY, FEDERAL FUNDING, AND REAUTHORIZING LEGISLATION

Garrine P. Laney and Alison Siskin

SUMMARY

On October 28, 2000, President Clinton signed into law the Violence Against Women Act (VAWA) of 2000 of Division B of the Victims of Trafficking and Violence Protection Act of 2000 (P.L. 106-386 (H.R. 3244)). VAWA 2000 reauthorized the Violence Against Women Act through FY2005, set new funding levels, and added new programs. The original Violence Against Women Act, enacted a Title IV of the Violent Crime Control and Law Enforcement Act (P.L. 1030322 (H.R. 3355)), became law in 1994.

For FY2003, President Bush requests $520 million for VAWA grant programs. His request would fund most VAWA programs at their authorized level. Among programs for which the Administration seeks funding, however, are two that are not authorized for FY2003 -- the Safe Havens for Children Pilot Program and Training Programs for Medical Personnel Who Perform Sexual Assault Forensic Exams.

Between FY1995 and FY1999, Congress steadily increased funding for mc of VAWA's grant programs. In FY2001, Congress appropriated $408 millic prior to the mandated rescission, for the programs that were authorized throu; VAWA 2000. In FY2002 to Congress appropriated $517.2 million for VAW programs, $7 million more than the amount requested in the President's budget.

VAWA established within the Departments of Justice (DOJ) and Health a: Human Services (HHS), a number of discretionary grant programs for state, loc and Indian tribal governments. DOJ administers VAWA grants designed to a law enforcement officers and prosecutors, encourage arrest policies, ste domestic violence and child abuse, establish and operate training programs f victim advocates and counselors, and train probation and parole officers who wo with released sex offenders. Under HHS, grants include funds for batter women's shelters, rape prevention and education, reduction of sexual abuse runaway and homeless street youth, and community programs on domes violence. Several studies of violent crimes against women were also mandated.

In addition to grants administered by the states, the act included a number changes in federal criminal law relating to interstate stalking, intrastate domes abuse, federal sex offense cases, the rules of evidence regarding use of a victim past sexual behavior, and HIV testing in rape cases.

VAWA 2000 reauthorized to most of the original act's programs and creat new grant programs to prevent sexual assaults on campuses, assistant victims violence with civil legal concerns, create transitional housing for victims domestic abuse, and enhance protections for elderly and disabled victims domestic violence. VAWA 2000, also, created a pilot program for safe custo exchange for families of domestic violence. Additionally, VAWA 20 authorized a number of studies on the effects of violence against women, creat domestic violence task force, and included changes in the federal criminal la relating to interstate stalking and immigration.

VIOLENCE AGAINST WOMEN:
BACKGROUND AND STATISTICS

Legislation proposing a federal response to the problem of violence agai; women was first introduced in 1990, although such violence was first identified a serious problem in the 1970s. Congressional action to address and gend related violence, culminated in the enactment of the Violence Against Women A (VAWA), which is Title IV of the Violent Crime Control and Law Enforcem

Act of 1994.[1] Funding under the bill emphasized enforcement as well as educational and social programs to prevent crime. The focus of the funding was on local government programs, an approach that the sponsors of the bill believed was the most promising technique for reducing crime and violence. They also cautioned that, due to the variety of programs funded through the states, the impact of the bill may be difficult to quantify.[2] Funding through FY2000 was authorized through the Violent Crime Reduction Trust Fund, created under Title XXXI of P.L. 103-322. Legislation to reauthorize VAWA though FY2005 was signed by the President on October 28, 2000 (P.L. 106-386).

Statistics on crimes of violence against women depict a personal safety problem that some believe may seriously limit the ability of threatened women to function fully in American society. Such crimes often have devastating consequences for these women personally, as well as for their families and for society as a whole. Since FY1995, VAWA has been a major source of funding for programs to reduce rape, stalking and domestic violence. The Departments of Justice (DOJ) and Health and Human Services (HHS), which administer the grant under VAWA, have produced a series of reports on the methods of assessing and preventing gender-related crimes. These reports, required by the statute, or submitted annually to Congress. The data collected under the VAWA are intended to help define the extent of the problem of violence against women and point towards possible solutions. The 1998 collaborative study of violence jointly funded by DOJ and HHS[3] reported that:

---

[1] P.L. 103-322; 108 Stat. 1902; 42 U.S.C. 13701.

[2] Indeed, there are only two studies that attempt to evaluate the overall defects of a VAWA grant program: (1) Martha R. Burt, Lisa C. Newmark, Lisa K. Jacobs, and Adele V. Harrell. *1998: Report: Evaluation of the STOP Formula Grants Under the Violence Against Women Act of 1994* (Washington, DC: Urban Institute, 1998); and (2) Neal Miller. *National Evaluation of the Arrest Policies Program Under VAWA*, presented at the Bureau of Justice Statistics/Justice Research Statistical Association National Conference in Minneapolis, MN, November 2, 2000. Though both studies provide examples of effective programs funded by the grants, neither study offers a conclusion as to the overall effectiveness of these grant programs.

[3] U.S. Department of Justice, National Institute of Justice, The office of Justice Programs, and Department of Health and Human Services, Center for Disease Control and Pre, Prevalence, Incidence and Consequences of Violence Against Women: Findings from the National Violence Against Women Survey (Washington: November 1998), p. 2. The principal source for crime data has long been the FBI's Uniform Crime Reporting Program, a compilation of monthly law enforcement reports and individual crime incident records voluntarily submitted. Since crimes against women are believed to be under-reported in the UCR, data for the collaborative DOJ-HHS survey were based on a nationally representative telephone survey of 8,000 women and 8,000 men. The survey was designed to protect confidentiality and minimize the potential for re-traumatizing victims. Differences in data collection methods explain the differences between the collaborative survey and the UCR.

- Using a definition of rape that includes forced vaginal, oral, and an intercourse, nearly 18% of women in the United States said they ha been raped (14.8%) or the victim of an attempted rape (2.8%) in the lifetime. Based on these survey figures, 17.7 million women a projected to have been raped. More than half of the rape victims said the were under 17 when first raped. Of the women who reported being rap at sometime in their lives, 22% were under 12 years old and 32% were to 17 years old when they were first raped.

- Differences in the prevalence of reported rape and physical assau among the women of different racial and ethnic backgrounds a statistically significant: American Indian/Alaska Native women we most likely to report these crimes, Asian/Pacific Island women were le likely to report them, and Hispanic women were less likely to make su reports than non-Hispanic women.

- Physical assault, ranging from slapping and hitting to gun violence, widespread: 52% of women said they were physically assaulted as a ch by an adult caretaker or as an adults by any type of perpetrator, and 1.9 of women said they were physically assaulted in the previous 12 month Based on the survey figures, approximately 1.9 million women a projected to be physically assaulted annually in the United States.

- Women report significantly more partner violence than do man: 25% women, compared with 8% of man, said they were raped or physical assaulted or both in their lifetime by a current or former spous cohabiting partner, or date; 1.5% of women and 0.9% of men said the were raped or physically assaulted by such a perpetrator in the previo 12 months. According to survey estimates, approximately 1.5 millic women and 834,700 men are projected to be raped or physical assaulted by an intimate partner annually in the United States.[4]

- Violence against adult women is primarily partner violence; 76% of t women (compared to 18% of men) who were raped physically assault or both since age 18 said the perpetrator was a current or former spous a co-habitating partner, or a date.

- Women are significantly more apt to be injured during an assault: 32% women and 16% of men who reported that they had been raped since a 18 said they were injured during their most recent rape. About one

---

[4] For men, the reported number of rate victims was insufficient to perform statistical tests significance.

three women who were injured during a physical assault required medical care.

- Stalking is more prevalent than previously thought. Using a definition of stalking that involves repeated visual or physical proximity, non-consensual communication, verbal, written or implied threats, or a combination of these that would cause a victim to feel a high level of fear, 8% of women and 2% of men said they were stalked at some time in their lives. One percent of the women and 0.4% of the men said they were stalked in the previous 12 months. According to survey estimates, approximately one million women and 371,000 men are projected to be stalked annually in the United States.

CHANGES IN FEDERAL CRIMINAL LAW

To help combat violence against women, the original VAWA rewrote several areas of federal criminal law. Penalties were created for interstate stalking or domestic abuse in cases where an abuser crossed a state line to injure or harass another, or forced a victim to cross a state line under duress and then physically harmed the victim in the course of a violent crime. Additionally, the law strengthened existing penalties for repeat sexual offenders and required restitution to victims and federal sex offense cases. VAWA called for pretrial detention and federal sex offense or child pornography felonies and allowed evidence of prior sex offenses to be used in some subsequent trials regarding federal sex crimes. The law also set new rules of evidence specifying that a victim's past sexual behavior generally was not admissible in federal civil or criminal cases regarding the sexual misconduct. Rape victims were allowed to demand that their alleged assailants tested for HIV, the virus that is generally believed to cause AIDS. A federal judge could order such a procedure after determining that risk to the victim existed

As in the original Act, VAWA 2000 created new stalking offenses, changing the law to create penalties for a person who travels in interstate or foreign commerce with the intent to kill, injure, or harass, or intimate a spouse or intimate partner, and who in the course of such travel commits or attempts to commit a crime of violence against the spouse or intimate partner. It also created penalties for a person who causes a spouse or intimate partner to travel in interstate or foreign commerce by force or coercion and in the course of such travel commits or tends to commit a crime of violence against the spouse or intimate partner. The

bill added the intimate partners of the victim as people covered under th
interstate stalking statute, and made it a crime to use the mail or any facility
interstate or foreign commerce to engage in a course of conduct that would place
person in reasonable fear of harm to themselves or their immediate family
intimate partner. Additionally, VAWA 2000 created penalties for any person wh
travels in interstate or foreign commerce with the intent of violating a protectic
order or causes a person to travel in interstate or foreign commerce by force
coercion and violates a protection order.[5]

CIVIL RIGHTS AND SUPREME COURT RULE[6]

Under Title IV, subtitle C -- "Civil Rights for Women," of the 1994 Ac
language was included that would have permitted private damage suits in feder
court by victims of "gender motivated violence." This provision was struck dov
(5-4) on May 15, 2000, by the Supreme Court in *United States v. Morrison*
unconstitutional under the Commerce Clause and the Fourteenth Amendmen
The Court fond that such violence did not substantially affect interstate commerc
It further noted that the Fourteenth Amendment is directed at state actions, n
those of private citizens. None of the other provisions of the 1994 Act have be
challenged in the Supreme Court.

GRANT PROGRAMS

Unaffected by the court decision were grant programs created by VAWA a
placed within DOJ and HHS. These programs are administered by the states a
funds can be allocated by the states to state agencies, Indian tribal governmen
units of local government and private nonprofit groups, and include grants
improve law enforcement and prosecution of violent crimes against wome
grants to encourage arrests in domestic violence incidents, moneys for rum
domestic violence and child abuse enforcement, rape prevention and educati
programs, and grants for battered women's shelters, among others. (A nation
domestic violence hotline is funded to a single contractor under the administrati

---

[5] P.L. 106-386., Section 1107.
[6] For a detailed analysis of *United States v. Morrison,* and its effect on VAWA, see CRS Rep
    RS20584, *united States v. Morrison: The Supreme Court Declares 42 U.S.C. Sec. 139*
    Unconstitutional, by T.J. Halstead, May 22, 2000.
[7] Nonetheless, victims can still bring damage suit in state courts.

of HHS.) The FY1995-FY2001 funding levels of these programs are listed in **Table 1.** Funding was authorized through FY2000 under the Violent Crime Reduction Trust Fund (VCRTF), created under Title XXXI of the Violent Crime Control and Law Enforcement Act of 1994. Authorization for VCRTF expired at the end of FY2000. Nonetheless, most of the programs in VAWA received appropriations for FY2001. (For a description of the grant programs in VAWA, see **Appendix A.**).[8]

REAUTHORIZING LEGISLATION

On October 28, 2000, President Clinton signed into law the Victims of Trafficking and Violence Protection Act of 2000 (P.L. 106-386; H.R. 3244/Smith), of which division B is the Violence Against Women Act of 2000. The Violence Against Women Act of 2000 continued to support VAWA by reauthorizing current programs and adding new initiatives including grants to assist victims of dating violence, transitional housing for victims of violence, a pilot program aimed at protecting children during visits with a parent who has been accused of domestic violence, and protections from violence for elderly and disabled women. It also made technical amendments, and required grant recipients to submit reports on the effectiveness of programs funded by the grants to aid with the dissemination of information on successful programs. The bill amended the Public Health Service Act (P.L. 98-457) to require that certain funds be used exclusively for rape prevention and education programs. Moreover, the bill made it easier for battered immigrant women to leave and to help prosecute their abusers. Under the old law, battered immigrant women could be deported if they leave abusers who are their sponsors for residency and citizenship in the United States. VAWA 2000 created special rules for alien battered spouses and children to allow them to remain in the United States.[9] (For a detailed listing of the new initiatives, please see Appendix B).

Actual appropriations for VAWA programs tend to be less than the amounts authorized in the bill. VAWA 2000 authorizes $3.2 billion for VAWA grant programs from FY2001 through FY2005: $667.5 million for FY2001, $642.3

---

[8] For detailed information on the grant programs and the application process, please consult the Department of Justice's Violence Against Women Office at [http://www.ojp.usdoj.gov/vawo/applicationkits.htm]. For information on grant programs in each state consult [http://www.ojp.usdoj.gov/vawo/stategrants.htm].

[9] See CRS Report RL30559, *Immigration: Noncitizen Victims of Family Violence*, by Andorra Bruno and Alison Siskin.

million for FY2002, $627.3 million for FY2003 and FY2004, $626.8 million i
FY2005. (See **Table 2.**)

FUNDING UNDER THE VIOLENCE AGAINST WOMEN ACT

For FY2003, President Bush requests $520 million for VAWA program
with $391 million for programs administered by the Department of Justice (DC
and $127 million for programs administered by the Department of Health a
Human Services (HHS.). As **Table 3** shows, the President's budget for FY20
requests funding at levels authorized for VAWA 2000 programs administered
DOJ, except that there is no funding request for Federal Victims Counselors or
Domestic Violence Task Force. The Administration has requested funding for
Safe Havens for Children Pilot Program and Training Programs for Medi
Personnel Who Perform Sexual Assault Forensic Exams, programs, which we
not authorized for FY2003. FY2003 funding request for VAWA Grants
Battered Women Shelters, administered by HHS, is $125 million, the sar
amount appropriated in FY2002. Authorized funding for this program in FY20
is $175 million.

In FY2002, funding appropriated for VAWA programs totaled $517.
million — VAWA programs administered by DOJ received a total of $390.
million, while VAWA programs under HHS received $126.62 million. With
HHS, the President requested funding for programs at FY2001 appropriatio
levels, and did not request monies for the transitional housing grant progra
created in VAWA 2000. The President also requested $44 million for ra
prevention and education grants; however, these grants were not specified
name in the Labor, Health and Human Services, and Education Appropriatio
Act of FY2002. Rather, the Administration proposed that funding for these gra
be included as part of Injury Prevention Grants. Congress provided $149.8 milli
for Injury Prevention Grants.

For FY2001, the President requested $481 million and Congress appropria
$407.1 million for VAWA programs, however, funding for VAWA progra
created in the original Act did not truly decrease from FY2000 appropriati
levels. Grants to Prevent Sexual Abuse of Runaway and Homeless Youth we
reauthorized in the Missing, Exploited, and Runway Children Protection Act (P
106-71) and received appropriations of $15 million, prior to the rescission,
FY2001. In addition, the Center for Disease Control received $176 million
prevention grants such as Rape Education and Prevention and Commun

Domestic Violence Programs, but the appropriations bill failed to specify amounts for the different programs. Assuming FY2001 funding levels for the prevention grants remained at FY2000 levels, funding for VAWA programs increased by almost $20 million between FY2000 and FY2001.[10] (The FY2000 amount enacted for VAWA programs was $435.75 million, $3 million less than the amount enacted for FY1999.[11]) As Table 1 shows, not all of the programs enacted under VAWA have been funded continuously; some have received money for a brief period only, while others have never been funded.

DEBATE OVER GENDER INCLUSIVENESS

Although the programs in the original VAWA law tended to be popular among criminal justice practitioners, and VAWA 2000 passed with almost unanimous support in Congress, VAWA did have its critics. Most of the criticisms of VAWA and VAWA 2000 came from those who felt that violence was a problem of both men and women, and that both men and women were victims of domestic violence. They argued that the programs in VAWA only addressed the needs of women victims.[12] Opponents of the law also felt that the legislation was paternalistic; it implied that women needed special protections.[13] Proponents of VAWA argued that the language of the law was gender-neutral and that programs could address the needs of men as well as women.[14]

---

[10] The Center for Disease Control reports that these grants received $45 million in FY2001.

[11] Consolidated Appropriations Act for FY2000 (P.L. 106-113) signed by President Clinton on Oct. 29, 1999. (See source note at end of table for complete Congressional Record citation.)

[12] For more information see the American Coalition for Fathers & Children homepage [http://www.acfc.org], visited on September 28, 2000.

[13] Gutmann, Stephanie. "Are All Men Rapists?" *National Review*, v. 45, August, 1993. p. 44-47. Young, Cathy. "Act Stirs Up Debate on Crime and Gender" Insight, v.9, November 29, 1993. p. 12-16.

[14] For more information see the National Coalition Against Domestic Violence homepage [http://www.ncadv.org], visited on October 10, 2000.

Table 1. Funds Appropriated for Violence against Women Grant Programs, FY1995-FY2001 (budget authority in millions of dollars)

Program	Admin agency	FY1995 enacted	FY1996 enacted	FY1997 enacted	FY1998 enacted	FY1999 enacted	FY2000 enacted	FY2001 enacted[a]
Law Enforcement and Prosecution Grants (STOP Grants) Section 40121)	OJP	26.00	130.00	145.00	172.00	206.75	206.75	209.72
Grant to Encourage Arrest Polices (Section 40231)	OJP	0.00	28.00	33.00	59.00	34.00	34.00	33.93
Rural Domestic Violence and Child Abuse Enforcement (Section 40295)	OJP	0.00	7.00	8.00	25.00	25.00	25.00	24.95
Court Appointed Special Advocates for Victims of Child Abuse (Section 40156a)	OJP	0.00	6.00	6.00	7.00	9.00	10.00	11.48
Training for Judicial Personnel and Practitioners for Victims of Child Abuse (Section 40156b)	OJP	0.00	0.75	1.00	2.00	2.00	2.00	1.95
Grants for Televised Testimony by Victims of Child Abuse (Section 1302)	OJP	0.00	0.05	0.55	1.00	1.00	1.00	1.00
National Stalker and Domestic Violence Reduction Grants (Section 1106)	OJP	0.00	1.50	1.75	2.75	0.00	0.00	0.00
Training Programs for Probation and Parole Officers Who Work With Under aged Sex Offenders (Section 40152)	OJP	0.00	1.00	1.00	2.00	5.00	5.00	5.00
National Study on Campus Sexual Assault (Section 40506)	OJP	0.00	0.00	.20	0.00	0.00	0.00	0.00
State Databases Studies (Section 40292)	OJP	0.00	0.20	0.00	0.00	0.00	0.00	0.00
Federal Victim Counselors (Section 40114)	USA	0.00	0.00	1.00	1.00	0.00	0.00	0.00
Total: Department of Justice		26.00	174.50	197.50	270.75	282.75	283.75	288.03
Training Judges/Court Personnel (Section 40421-22)	N/A	0.00	0.00	0.00	0.00	0.00	0.00	0.00
Total: The Judiciary		0.00	0.00	0.00	0.00	0.00	0.00	0.00

Program	Admin agency	FY1995 enacted	FY1996 enacted	FY1997 enacted	FY1998 enacted	FY1999 enacted	FY2000 enacted	FY2001 enacted[a]
Courts/Training Grants (Section 40411-14)								
Total: State Justice Institute		0.00	.00	0.00	0.00	0.00	0.00	0.00
National Domestic Violence Hotline (Section 40211)	ACF	1.00	0.00	1.20	1.20	1.20	2.00	2.16
Grants to Reduce Sexual Abuse of Runaway, Homeless, and Street Youth (Section 40155)	ACF	0.00	5.56	8.00	15.00	15.00	15.00	15.00[b]
Grants for Battered Women Shelters (Section 40241)	ACF	0.00	15.00	10.80	76.80	88.80	101.50	116.92
National Number and Cost of Injuries Study (Section 40293)	CDC	0.00	0.10	0.00	0.00	0.00	0.00	0.00
Rape Prevention and Education Grants (Section 40151)	CDC	0.00	28.54	35.00	45.00	45.00	45.00	c
Community Programs on Domestic Violence (Section 40261)	CDC	1.00	3.00	6.00	6.00	6.00	6.00	c
Total: Department of Health and Human Services		1.00	52.60	51.00	144.00	156.00	169.50	119.08
Grant Total		27.00	227.10	258.50	420.75	438.75	453.25	407.11

Sources: For FY1995–FY2000 funding information, see *Budget of the United States Government: Appendix* for indicated y ears under named agencies. FY2001: Commerce, Justice State Appropriations (P.L. 106-553) signed into law on December 21, 2000. FY2001: Labor, Health and Human Services, and Education Appropriations (P.L. 106-554) signed into law on December 21, 2000.

[a] The FY2001 Consolidated Appropriations Act (P.L. 106-554) contained a provision mandating a 0.22 percent government-wide rescission of discretionary budget authority for FY2001 for all government agencies (except for certain defense activities). The amounts appropriated for FY2001 in the table include the rescission.

[b] These grants were reauthorized FY2003 by the Missing, Exploited, and Runaway Children Protection Act (P.L. 106-71; S. 249/Hatch), which was signed into law on October 12, 1999. Thus, these monies are not included in the total of VAWA funds for FY2001.

[c] These grants were not specified by name in the appropriations bill. In H.R. 4577, however, the CDC was allocated $175.97 million for injury prevention grants, which would include these programs. The House Appropriations Committee report mentioned that $45 million should be appropriated for rape prevention grants, however, this language was not included in the bill.

Abbreviations to table: In DOJ: USA (United States Attorneys), OJP (Office of Justice Programs)

In HHS: ACF (Administration for Children and Families), CDC (Centers for Disease Control and Prevention)

Table 2. Funding Authorized in the Violence Against Women Act 2000 (P.L. 106-386) ($ in millions)

Program	Admin. agency	FY2001	FY2002	FY2003	FY2004	FY2005
Law Enforcement and Prosecution (STOP) Grants (Section 1102-1103)	OJP	185.00	185.00	185.00	185.00	185.00
Grants to Encourage Arrest Policies (Section 1104)	OJP	65.00	65.00	65.00	65.00	65.00
Rural Domestic Violence and Child Abuse Enforcement (Section 1105)	OJP	40.00	40.00	40.00	40.00	40.00
Court Appointment Special Advocates for Victims of Child Abuse (Section 1302)	OJP	12.00	12.00	12.00	12.00	12.00
Training for Judicial Personnel and Practitioners for Victims of Child Abuse (Section 1302)	OJP	2.30	2.30	2.30	2.30	2.30
Grants for Televised Testimony by Victims of Child Abuse (Section 1302)	OJP	1.00	1.00	1.00	1.00	1.00
National Stalker and Domestic Violence Reduction Grants (Section 1106)	OJP	3.00	3.00	3.00	3.00	3.00
Training Programs for Law Enforcement Officers on Elder Abuse, Neglect, and Exploitation (Section 1209)	OJP	5.00	5.00	5.00	5.00	5.00
Civil and Legal Assistance for Victims of Violence (Section 1201)	OJP	40.00	40.00	40.00	40.00	40.00
Safe Havens for Children Pilot Program (Section 1301)	OJP	15.00	15.00	0.00	0.00	0.00
Grants to Decrease Violence Against Women with Disabilities (Section 1402)	OJP	7.50	7.50	7.50	7.50	7.50
Training Programs for Medical Personnel who Perform Sexual Assault Forensic Exams (Section 1405)	OJP	.20	0.00	0.00	0.00	0.00
Domestic Violence Task Force (Section 1407)	OJP	.50	.50	.50	.50	.50
Federal Victim Counselors (Section 1205)	USA	1.00	1.00	1.00	1.00	1.00
Subtotal: Department of Justice		377.50	377.30	362.30	362.30	361.80

Program	Admin. agency	FY2001	FY2002	FY2003	FY2004	FY2005
Training Judges/Court Personnel (Section 1204)	N/A	.50	.50	.50	.50	.50
Subtotal: The Judiciary		.50	.50	.50	.50	.50
Equal Justice for Women in Courts/Training Grants (Section 1406(a))	N/A	1.5	1.5	1.5	1.5	1.5
Subtotal: State Justice Institute		1.5	1.5	1.5	1.5	1.5
National Domestic Violence Hotline (Section 1204)	ACF	2.00	2.00	2.00	2.00	2.00
Grants for Battered Women Shelters (Section 1202)	ACF	175.00	175.00	175.00	175.00	175.00
Transitional Housing for Victims of Domestic Violence (Section 1203)	ACF	25.00	0.00	0.00	0.00	0.00
Rape Prevention and Education Grants (Section 1402)	CDC	80.00	80.00	80.00	80.00	80.00
Community Programs on Domestic Violence (Section 1403)	CDC	6.00	6.00	6.00	6.00	6.00
Subtotal: Department of Health and Human Services		288.00	263.00	263.00	263.00	263.00
Grant Total		667.50	642.30	627.30	627.30	626.80

Source: Violence Against Women Act of 2000 (P.L. 106-386) as signed by the President on October 28, 2000.

Note: Section numbers refer to P.L. 106-386.

List of Abbreviations.

Within DOJ: USA: United States Attorneys, OJP: Office of Justice Programs

Within HHS: ACF: Administration for Children and Families, CDC: Centers for Disease Control and Prevention

Table 3. Funding Authorized in the Violence Against Women Act 2000 (P.L. 106-386) for FY2003, Appropriations for FY2002, and Amounts Requested in the President's FY2003 Budget ($ in millions)

Program	Admin. agency	FY2002 enacted	Authoriz. FY2003	Request FY2003
Law Enforcement and Prosecution (STOP) Grants (Section 1102-1103)	OJP	184.74	185.00	185.00
Grants to Encourage Arrest Policies (Section 1104)	OJP	64.93	65.00	65.00
Rural Domestic Violence and Child Abuse Enforcement (Section 1105)	OJP	39.95	40.00	40.00
Court Appointment Special Advocates for Victims of Child Abuse (Section 1302)	OJP	11.98	12.00	12.00
Training for Judicial Personnel and Practitioners for Victims of Child Abuse (Section 1302)	OJP	2.30	2.30	2.30
Grants for Televised Testimony by Victims of Child Abuse (Section 1302)	OJP	1.00	1.00	1.00
National Stalker and Domestic Violence Reduction Grants (Section 1106)	OJP	3.00	3.00	3.00
Training Programs for Probation and Parole Officers Who Work With Released Sex Offenders (Section not included in VAWA 2000)	OJP	5.00	—[a]	5.00
Grants to Reduce Crimes Against Women on Campus (Section 1108)	OJP	10.00	[b]	10.00
Training Programs for Law Enforcement Officers on to Enhance Protections Against Elder Abuse, Neglect, and Exploitation (Section 1209)	OJP	5.00	5.00	5.00
Civil and Legal Assistance for Victims of Violence (Section 1201)	OJP	40.00	40.00	40.00
Safe Havens for Children Pilot Program (Section 1301)	OJP	15.00	0.00	15.00
Grants to Decrease Violence Against Women with Disabilities (Section 1402)	OJP	7.50	7.50	7.50
Training Programs for Medical Personnel who Perform Sexual Assault Forensic Exams (Section 1405)	OJP	.20	0.00	.20
Report on Parental Kidnapping (Section 1303)	OJP	0.00	0.00	0.00
Domestic Violence Task Force (Section 1407)	OJP	0.00	1.00	0.00
Federal Victim Counselors (Section 1205)	USA	0.00	1.00	0.00
Subtotal: Department of Justice		390.60	362.30	391.00

Program	Admin. agency	FY2002 enacted	Authoriz. FY2003	Request FY2003
Training Judges/Court Personnel (Section 1406(b))	N/A	0.00	.50	0.50
Subtotal: State Justice Institute		0.00	1.5	1.50
National Domestic Violence Hotline (Section 1204)	ACF	2.16	2.00	2.00
Grants for Battered Women Shelters (Section1202)	ACF	124.46	175.00	125.00
Transitional Housing for Victims of Domestic Violence (Section 1203)	ACF	0.00	0.00	0.00
Rape Prevention and Education Grants (Section 1402)	CDC	c	80.00	d
Community Programs on Domestic Violence (Section 1403)	CDC	c	6.00	d
Subtotal: Department of Health and Human Services		126.62	263.00	127.00
Grand Total		517.22	627.30	520.00

Sources: Violence Against Women Act of 2000 (P.L. 106-386) as signed by the President on October 28, 2000. For FY2003 budget request, see *Budget of the United States Government: Appendix* under named agencies. FY2002 Commerce, Justice, State Appropriations (P.L. 107-77) signed into law on November 28, 2001. FY2002: Labor, Health and Human Services, and Education Appropriations (P.L. 107-116) signed into law on January 10, 2002.

Note: Section numbers refer to P.L. 106-386.

[a] VAWA 2000 did not reauthorize training programs for probation and parole officers who work with released sex offenders.

[b] VAWA 2000 authorized "such sums as may be necessary" for grants to reduce crimes against women on campuses.

[c] These grants were not specified by name in the FY2002: Labor, Health and Human service, and Education Appropriations Act (P.L. 107-116). In FY2002, the Administration proposed that funding for these grants be included as part of Injury Prevention Grants. Congress provided $149.77 million for Injury Prevention Grants.

[d] Grants for rape prevention and education and community programs on domestic violence were not given a separate line number in the President's budget.

APPENDIX A: DESCRIPTION OF GRANT PROGRAMS

Law Enforcement and Prosecution (Special Training Officers and Prosecutors (STOP)) Grants

The purpose of STOP grants, administered by the Attorney General, is to help state governments, Indian tribal governments, and units of local government strengthen law enforcement, prosecution, and victims' services in cases involving violent crimes against women. These grants may be used to provide personnel, training, technical assistance, data collection, and other equipment to increase the apprehension, prosecution, and adjudication of persons committing violent crimes against women. Activities may include:

- training law enforcement officers and prosecutors to more effectively identify and respond to violent crimes against women, including those of sexual assault, domestic violence, and dating violence;
- developing, training, or expanding units of law enforcement officers and
- prosecutors specifically targeting violent crimes against women;
- developing and implementing more effective police and prosecution policies, protocols, orders, and services specifically devoted to preventing, identifying and responding to violent crimes against women;
- developing, installing, or expanding relevant data collection and communication systems;
- developing, enlarging, or strengthening programs for relevant victim services to address stalking and to address the needs and circumstances of Indian tribes in dealing with violent crimes against women including dating violence;
- developing, enlarging, or strengthening programs to assist law enforcement and the courts to address the needs of older individuals and individuals with disabilities who are the victims of domestic violence and sexual assault;
- coordinating the response of state law enforcement agencies, prosecutors, courts, victim service agencies, and other state agencies to violence crimes against women, including dating violence; and

- training of sexual assault forensic medical personnel in the collection and
- preservation of evidence, analysis, prevention, and providing expert testimony and treatment of trauma related to sexual assault.

At least 25% of each grant must be allotted, without duplication, 1.0 each of three areas, respectively: prosecution, law enforcement, and victim services. Of the amounts appropriated: 5% is allocated to Indian tribal governments; $600,000 is available for grants to applicants in each state; 5% of the funds must be set aside for state sexual assault and domestic violence coalitions; and the remaining funds are to be distributed to applicants in each state on the basis of relative population. For more information see [http://www.ojp.usdoj.gov/vawo/grants/stop/descrip.htm]. [Section 40121]

State Domestic Violence and Sexual Assault Coalition Grants

These grants are distributed by the Attorney General for state domestic violence and sexual assault coalitions. Such coalitions shall further the purposes of domestic violence or sexual assault intervention and prevention through information and training. Each state, the District of Columbia, Puerto Rico, and the combined U.S. Territories should receive 1/53rd of the funds allocated. 2.5% of the STOP funds are set aside, each, for state sexual assault and domestic violence coalitions.

Rape Prevention and Education Grants

The funds for these grants are added to the Preventive Health Services Block Grants monies already distributed to the states by the Department of Health and Human Services. The grants may he used by the states for rape prevention and education programs conducted by rape crisis centers or similar non-governmental nonprofit entities. Specifically, these grants may be used for:

- educational seminars
- operation of rape crisis hotlines
- training programs for professionals
- the preparation of training materials

- education and training for students and campus personnel
- education to increase awareness about drugs used to facilitate rapes or sexual assaults
- other efforts to increase awareness or prevent sexual assault especially in under-served communities.

Of the monies provided to the states 25% must be used for education in middle, junior high, and high schools. Grants are made on the basis of the relative population of each state. [Section 40151-152]

National Domestic Violence Hotline

These funds are authorized for the Secretary of Health and Human Services to make a grant to a private, non-profit entity to provide for the operation of a national, toll-free telephone hotline to provide information and assistance to victims of domestic violence. The grant may fund the use and operation of the telephone line; the employment, training, and supervision of personnel to answer calls and provide counseling and referral services on a 24-hour basis; the establishment of a database with information and services available for victims of domestic violence; and the advertisement of the hotline to potential users nationwide. [Section 40211]

Grants to Encourage Arrests Policies in Domestic Violence Cases

The purpose of these grants is to assist state governments, Indian tribal governments, and units of local government in treating domestic violence as a serious violation of criminal law. Grants may be used to:

- implement mandatory arrest or pro-arrest programs and policies in police departments;
- develop policies and training in police departments to improve tracking of cases involving domestic violence and dating violence;
- centralize and coordinate police enforcement, prosecution, or judicial responsibility for domestic violence cases;
- coordinate computer tracking systems to ensure communication between police, prosecutors, and the courts;

- strengthen legal advocacy service programs for victims of domestic violence and dating violence;
- develop or strengthen policies and training for the police, prosecutors, and the judiciary in recognizing, investigating, and prosecuting instances of domestic violence and sexual assault against older individuals and individuals with disabilities; and
- educate judges about domestic violence and improve judicial handling of such cases.

Applicants must certify that their laws or official policies encourage or mandate arrest policies in domestic violence cases and do not require the abused to bear the costs associated with the filing of criminal charges. Priority is given to applicants who do not currently provide for centralized handling of cases involving domestic violence by police, prosecutors, and the courts, and to those who demonstrate a commitment to strong enforcement and prosecution of such cases. For more information consult [http://www.ojp.usdoj.gov/vawo/grants/arrest/descrip.htm]. [Section 40231]

Grants for Battered Women's Shelters

These grants are distributed by the Secretary of Health and Human Services for battered women's shelters. The grants for each state are allocated based on the relative population of the state except that: (1) each state is allocated not less than 1% of the total grant or $600,000 which ever is less; and (2) Guam, American Samoa, the Virgin Islands, the Northern Mariana Islands, and the Trust Territory of the Pacific Islands are allotted not less than one-eighth of 1% of the amounts available for grants. [Section 40241]

Community Programs on Domestic Violence

These grants are provided by the Secretary of Health and Human Services to non-profit private organizations for the purpose of establishing projects in local communities to coordinate intervention and prevention efforts against domestic violence.

Grants will fund local projects that coordinate efforts among such sectors as health care providers, the education community, the religious community, the criminal justice system, human service entities, and business and civic leaders. Grants may be made for up to 3 years and are to be geographically dispersed throughout the country. [Section 40261]

National Stalker and Domestic Violence Reduction Grants

Provides authority for the Attorney General to make grants to state and units of local government to improve data entry for cases of stalking and domestic violence in local, state, and national crime information databases most notably the National Crime Information Center (NCIC).

Applicants must certify that they have established a program that enters into the NCIC records of:

- warrants for the arrest of persons violating protection orders intended to protect victims from stalking and domestic violence;
- arrests or convictions of persons violating protection or domestic violence; and
- protection orders for the protection of persons from stalking and domestic violence.

These grants are awarded on a need-based basis for entities that do not have this type of system in place. [Sections 40602-607]

Rural Domestic Violence and
Child Abuse Enforcement Grants

These grants are provided by the Attorney General to states, Indian tribal governments, or local governments of rural states, and to other public and private entities of rural states to (1) implement, expand and establish cooperative efforts and projects between law enforcement officers, prosecutors, victim advocacy groups, and other related parties to investigate and prosecute incidents of domestic violence, dating violence, and child abuse; (2) provide treatment and counseling to such victims; and (3) work cooperatively to develop education and prevention strategies at the community level. A minimum of 5% of the grant monies are allocated to Indian tribal government. For more information see [http://www.ojp.usdoj.gov/vawo/grants/rural/descrip.htm]. [Section 40295]

Victims of Child Abuse Grants

VAWA amended the Victims of Child Abuse Act of 1990 to provide authorization for three purposes:

- the court-appointed special advocate program;
- child abuse training programs for judicial personnel and practitioners; and
- grants for televised testimony.

Priority for the court-appointed special advocate program grants are given to localities that do not have existing programs and to programs in need of expansion. Priority for child abuse training programs are given to programs that aim to improve the procedures of child service agencies.

Federal Victims Counselors

This money is allocated to the U.S. Attorneys to appoint victims/witness counselors for prosecution of sex and domestic violence crimes where applicable. [Section 40114]

Grants to Reduce Sexual Abuse of Runaway, Homeless, and Street Youth

The Secretary of Health and Human Services may make grants to private, non-profit agencies for prevention of sexual abuse and exploitation of runaway, homeless, and street youth. Funds may be used for street-based outreach and education, including treatment, counseling, provision of information and referrals for those subject to or at risk of sexual abuse. Priority is given to those agencies with experience in providing services to this population. These grant were reauthorized through FY2003 by the Missing, Exploited, and Runway Children Protection Act (P.L. 106-71; S. 249/Hatch), which was signed into law on October 12, 1999. [Section 40155]

Equal Justice for Women in the Courts

The State Justice Institute and the Federal Judicial Center, respectively, may make grants to provide model programs involving training of judges and court personnel in state and federal courts on rape, sexual assault, domestic violence, and other gender motivated crimes.

The State Justice Institute grants may be used to train Indian tribal judges and court personnel in the laws on rape, sexual assault, domestic violence, dating violence, and other crimes of violence motivated by the victim's gender. The funds may also be used for training on the issues raised by domestic violence and sexual assault in determining custody and visitation. At least 40% of funds must be expended on model programs regarding domestic violence and at least 40% of funds must be expended on model programs regarding rape and sexual assault.

The Federal Judicial Center grants may be used to educate and train judges on issues related to gender bias in the courts. [Sections 40411-414, 40421-422].

APPENDIX B: NEW INITIATIVES IN THE VIOLENCE AGAINST WOMEN ACT 2000

Grant Programs

Grants for Legal Assistance to Victims

VAWA 2000 authorizes the Attorney General to award grants to private nonprofit entities, Indian tribal governments, and publically funded organizations to increase the availability of legal assistance to victims of domestic violence, stalking, or sexual assault in legal matters, such as immigration, housing matters, and protection orders, at minimum or no cost to the victim. These grants may be used to establish or expand cooperative efforts between victim services organizations and legal assistance providers, by providing training, technical assistance, and data collection. [Section 1201]

Short Term Transitional Housing

VAWA 2000 includes grants for short- term transitional housing assistance and support services for victims of domestic abuse. These grants are administered by the Secretary of HHS. [Section 1203]

Older and Disabled Individuals

VAWA 2000 amends the language of STOP grants and "Grants to Encourage Arrest Policies" to provide funds to increase protection of older individuals and individuals with disabilities from domestic violence and sexual assault through policies and training for police, prosecutors, and the judiciary. It also creates new grants, administered by the Attorney General, for training programs to assist law enforcement officers, prosecutors, and court officials in addressing, investigating and prosecuting instances of elder abuse, neglect, and exploitation, and violence against individuals with disabilities, including domestic violence and sexual assault. VAWA 2000 authorizes $5 million annually, FY2001-FY2005 for grants for these training programs. [Section 1209]

Safe Haven Pilot Program

VAWA 2000 authorizes the Attorney General to award grants to state, local, and Indian tribal governments to provide supervised visitation and safe visitation exchange for children involved in situations of domestic violence, child abuse, or sexual assault. [Section 1301]

Other Initiatives

Studies

There are several studies authorized in VAWA 2000. These include studies of: (1) insurance discrimination against victims of domestic violence; (2) workplace effects of violence against women; (3) unemployment compensation for women who are victims of violence; and (4) parental kidnapping. VAWA 2000 also requires the National Institute of Justice (Nil) to develop a research agenda and plans to implement the agenda based on the National Academy of Sciences' recommendations in the report Understanding Violence Against Women. [Sections 1206-1208, 1303-1304]

Battered Immigrant Women Protection Act of 2000

VAWA 2000 contains the Battered Immigrant Women Protection Act of 2000, which provides for increased protection of immigrant women who are victims of domestic abuse, and creates special rules for alien battered spouses and children to allow them to remain in the United States.[15] [Sections 1501-1513]

---

[15] See CRS Report RL30559, *Immigration: Noncitizen Victims of Family Violence*, by Andorra Bruno and Alison Siskin.

Dating Violence

VAWA 2000 defines "dating violence" as:

> violence committed by a person (A) who is or has been in a social relationship of a romantic or intimate nature with the victim; and (B) where the existence of such a relationship shall be determined based on a consideration of the following factors: (1) the length of the relationship; (ii) the type of relationship; and (iii) the frequency of interaction between the persons involved in the relationship.

VAWA 2000 amends the original law so that STOP grants, grants to encourage arrest policies, and rural domestic violence grants can be awarded for programs to combat "dating violence." [Section 1109]

Task Force on Domestic Violence

VAWA 2000 also establishes a task force to coordinate research on domestic violence. [Section 1407]

Chapter 5

VIOLENCE AGAINST WOMEN: FEDERAL FUNDING AND RECENT DEVELOPMENTS

Suzanne Cavanagh and David Teasley

SUMMARY

According to a newly designed Bureau of Justice Statistics survey, "women annually reported about 500,000 rapes and sexual assaults....." Legislation proposing a federal response to the problem of violence against women was first introduced in 1990. Over the next several years, congressional actions to address public concerns about this problem culminated in the enactment of new penalties under the Violent Crime Control and Law Enforcement Act of 1994, and the establishment of several grant programs under its Title IV, the Violence Against Women Act (P.L. 103-322). In FY 1996, Congress approved VAWA funding for selected programs, including the Department of Justice ($175 million); and the Department of Health and Human Services ($54 million). In FY 1997, Congress approved VAWA funding for the selected programs, including the Department of Justice ($197.5 million), and the Department of Health and Human Services ($61 million).

VIOLENCE AGAINST WOMEN:
RECENT DEVELOPMENTS

The Justice Department has released new and more accurate data about the extent of violence against women. Since 1994, a major source of funding has been grant programs authorized by the Violence Against Women Act (P.L. 103-322, Title IV) and funded in FY1995.[1]

Statistics

Over two years ago, the Department of Justice's Bureau of Justice Statistics (BJS) redesigned the *National Crime Victimization Survey (NCVS)* to obtain a more accurate reporting of incidents of rape and sexual assault. The *NCVS* obtains data about criminal activity from a nationally representative sample of U.S. households. Each year, interviews are conducted of every person aged 12 and over in these households to measure crime from the victim's perspective. This approach differs from that of the Federal Bureau of Investigation's *Uniform Crime Reports (UCR),* which is based solely on crimes reported to the police. BJS statisticians caution that the redesign of the survey means that the data "are not directly comparable to earlier estimates."[2] In addition, they note that despite their effort to obtain that new information, those women surveyed may still be reluctant to provide information due to "the private nature of the event, the perceived stigma and the belief that no purpose would be served in reporting the crime ...."[3]

Based upon a nationally representative sample of U.S. households, the B.J.S. reported the following findings:

- "Women age 12 or older annually sustained almost 5 million violent victimizations in 1992 and 1993. About three-quarters of all lone-offender violence against women and 45 percent of violence multiple-offenders was perpetrated by offenders whom the victim

---

[1] For background information on violence against women, see : U.S. Library of Congress. Congressional Research Service. *Violence Against Women: An Overview.* CRS Report 94-142 GOV, by Suzanne Cavanagh, Leslie Gladstone and David Teasley. Washington 1994. 19 p.; and *Domestic Violence Data, Federal Programs, and Selected Issues.* CRS Report 95-865 EPW, by Dale Robinson. Washington 1995. 12 p.

[2] U.S. Department of justice. Pres Release: Women Usually Victimized by Offenders They Know. August 16, 1995. p. 3.

[3] Ibid., p. 4.

knew. In 29 percent of all violence against women by a lone offender, the perpetrator was an intimate (husband, ex-husband, boyfriend or ex-boyfriend).

- Women were about six times more likely than men to experience violence committed by an intimate

- Women annually reported about 500,000 rapes and sexual assaults to interviewers. Friends or acquaintances of the victims committed over half of these rapes were sexual assaults. Strangers were responsible for about 1 in 5.

- Women of all races were about equally vulnerable to violence by an intimate.

- Among the victims of violence committed by an intimate, the victimization rate of women separated from their husbands was about three times higher than that of divorced women and about 25 times higher than that of married women. Because the *NCVS* reflects a respondent's marital status at that time of the interview, which is up to six months after the incident, it is possible that separation or divorce followed the violence.

- Female victims of violence by intimate were more and often injured by the violence and than females victimized by a stranger."[4]

The *UCR* reported 102,100 forcible rapes in 1994, a 3.7% decrease from the previous year. Between 1990 and 1994, the number of known rape offenses decreased by -0.4%.[5] Also, during 1994, 4,739 women were victims of murder, of which 823 were murdered by their husbands and 525 were murdered by boyfriends.[6]

LEGISLATION

Legislation proposing a federal response to the problem of violence against women was first introduced in 1990. Over the next several years, congressional actions to address public concerns about this problem,

---

[4] Quoted from U.S. Department of Justice. Bureau of Justice Statistics. *Violence against women: Estimates from the Redesigned Survey.* Washington, August 1995. p. 1.

[5] U.S. Department of Justice. Federal Bureau of Investigation. *Uniform Crime Reports, 1993.* Washington, U.S. Govt. Print. Off., 1995. p. 58.

[6] Ibid, pp. 16, 19.

culminated in the enactment of new penalties under the Violent Crime Control and Law Enforcement Act of 1994, and the establishment of several grant programs under its Title IV, the Violence Against Women Act (P.L. 103-322).[7]

FY1995 Funding Under the Violence Against Women Act

The Violence Against Women Act creates a number of new grant programs.[8] Within the Department of Justice's National Institute of Justice, a new Violence Against Women Office was created to administer these programs, with former Iowa Attorney General Bonnie Campbell as director.[9]

In FY1995, the Violence Against Women Act (VAWA) received an appropriation of $1 million for the National Domestic Violence Hotline, to be administered by the Department of Health and Human Services. In addition, the Department of Justice (DoJ) will administer an appropriation of $26 million, to be used for law enforcement, prosecution and victim services grants to reduce violence against women.

On March 21,1995, DoJ announced the initiation of the STOP-- Services, Training, Officers, Prosecutors -- Violence Against Women Formula Grant Program. As of April 1996, DoJ has awarded approximately $426,000 to each state. Funds are to be distributed upon receipt of the various states' implementation plans. Funds are to be allocated as follows: 25% to law enforcement, 25% to prosecution, and 25% to nonprofit victims services. The rest is to be allocated at the state's discretion but within the parameters of the Act.

States must (1) certified that all out-of-pocket costs for forensic medical examinations of victims of sexual assaults are paid by the state, local government, or other government entity; (2) certify that victims of domestic violence are exempt from paying costs associated with filing criminal charges or issuing or serving a warrant, protection order, or witness subpoena for a domestic violence offense; and (3) assure that it will be in

---

[7] See: U.S. Library of Congress. Congressional Research Service. Crime Control: Summary of the Violent Crime Control and Law Enforcement Act of 1994. Report No. 94-910. Coordinated by Charles Doyle. Washington 1994. pp. 32-48.

[8] Ibid. pp. 32-38.

[9] Justice Information Electronic Newsletter, Vol. 1. April 1, 1995. Program guidelines and application kits may be obtained from the Department of Justice Response Center, 1-800-421-6770.

compliance with the above requirements by Sept. 13, 1996 or at the end of the next legislative session, whichever is later.[10]

Recent Developments Within the 104th Congress

With the completion of the FY1996 appropriations process, Congress has approved funding for several programs under the Violence against Women Act. Congress approved FY1996 funding for selected programs, including, but not limited to, the Department of Justice's Office of Justice Programs ($175 million); and in the Department of Health and Human Services' Administration for Children and Families, and the Public Health Service ($54 million).

Signed into law by President Clinton on September 30, 1996, the Omnibus Consolidated Appropriations Act, 1997 (H.R. 3610; P.L. 104 -- XXXX, number not yet assigned) provides VAWA FY 1997 funding for selected programs, including, but not limited to, the Department of Justice ($197.5 million), and the Department of Health and Human Services ($61 million).

---

[10] Ibid.

Table 1. Violence Against Women Program Funding, FY1995-FY1997 (budget authority in millions)

Program	Admin. Agency	FY1995 Enacted	FY1996 Request	FY1996 Enacted	FY1997 Request	FY1997 Enacted
Law Enforcement and Prosecution Grants (Sec. 40121)	OJP	26.00	130.00	130.00	145.00	145.00
Grants to Encourage Arrest Policies (Sec. 40231)	OJP	0	28.00	28.00	33.00	33.00
Rural Domestic Violence and Child Abuse Enforcement (Sec. 40295)	OJP	0	7.00	7.00	8.00	8.00
Court Appointed Special Advocates for Victims of Child Abuse (Sec. 40156a)	OJP	0	6.00	6.00	6.00	6.00
Training for Judicial Personnel and Practitioners for Victims of Child Abuse (Sec. 40156b)	OJP	0	0.75	0.75	1.00	1.00
Grants for Televised Testimony by Victims of Child Abuse (Sec. 40156c)	OJP	0	0.25	0.05	0.55	0.55
National Stalker and Domestic Violence Reduction Grants (Sec. 40603)	OJP	0	1.50	1.50	1.75	1.75
Training Programs for Probation and Parole Officers Who Work With Released Sex Offenders (Sec. 40152)	OJP	0	1.00	1.00	1.00	1.00
National Study on Campus Sexual Assault (Sec. 40506)	OJP	0	0.20	0	0.20	0.20
State Databases Studies	OJP	0	0.20	0.20	0	0
Federal Victim Counselors	USA	0	0.50	0	1.00	1.00
Subtotal: Department of Justice		26.00	175.40	175.40	197.50	197.50

Program	Admin. Agency	FY1995 Enacted	FY1996 Request	FY1996 Enacted	FY1997 Request	FY1997 Enacted
Training Judges/Court Personnel (Sec. 40421-22)		0	0.70	0	0	0
Subtotal: The Judiciary		0	0.70	0	0	0
Equal Justice for Women in Courts/Training Grants (Sec. 40411-14)		0	0.60	0	0	0
Subtotal: State Justice Institute		0	0.60	0	0	0
National Domestic Violence Hotline (Sec. 40211).	ACF	1.00	0.40	0.40	0.40	1.20
Grants to Reduce Sexual Abuse of Runaway, Homeless, and Street Youth (Sec. 40155)	ACF	0	7.00	5.56	8.00	8.00
Grants for Battered Women Shelters (Sec. 40241)	ACF	0	15.00	15.00	27.38	10.80
Youth Education and Domestic Violence (Sec. 40251)	ACF	0	0.40	0.40	0	0
National Number and Cost of Injuries Study (Sec. 40151	CDC	0	0.10	0.10	0	0
Rape Prevention and Education Grants (Sec. 40151)	CDC	0	35.00	28.54	35.00	35.00
Community Programs on Domestic Violence (Sec. 40261)	CDC	0	4.00	3.00	6.00	6.00
Subtotal: Department of Health and Human Services		1.00	61.90	54.00	76.78	61.00
Safety for Women: Capital Improvements to Prevent Crime in National Parks (Sec. 40132)		0	5.00	0	0	0
Safety for Women: Capital Improvements to Prevent Crime in Public Parks (Sec. 40133)		0	7.50	0	0	0
Subtotal: Department of the Interior		0	12.50	0	0	0

Program	Admin. Agency	FY1995 Enacted	FY1996 Request	FY1996 Enacted	FY1997 Request	FY1997 Enacted
Safety for Women: Capital Improvements to Prevent Crime in Public Transportation (Sec. 40131)		0	5.00	0	0	0
Subtotal: Department of Transportation		0	5.00	0	0	0

Source: The Omnibus Consolidated Appropriations Act, 1997 (H.R. 3610; P.L. 104-XXX, number not yet assigned) conference report (H. Rept. 104-863), as provided in the *Congressional Record*, September 28, 1996, vol. 142, no. 137, p. H11644 *ff*.

Abbreviations to TABLE 1.
ACF   Administration for Children and Families
CDC   Centers for Disease Control
OJP   Office of Justice Programs
USA   United States Attorneys

Note: This table originally appeared in the following CRS report. U.S. Library Congress. Congressional Research Service. Domestic Violence: Data, Federal Programs, and Selected Issues. CRS Report 95-865 EPW, by Dale Robinson. Washington, August 3, 1995.

Chapter 6

WELFARE REFORM:
DOMESTIC VIOLENCE VICTIMS

Vee Burke

ISSUE

How should victims of domestic violence be treated under TANF? What steps would they take toward self-sufficiency? Should they be excused from requirements to work? TANF law gives states an option, known as the Family Violence Option, to waive normal program requirements for mothers who have suffered domestic violence. The purpose of this provision of the 19996 law is to enable states to help victims of domestic violence without subjecting them to TANF rules that might "unfairly penalize" them or put them at risk of further abuse.

BACKGROUND

The Family Violence Option

The Family Violence Option (FVO) is an *optional* certification in a state TANF plan specifying that the state has established an is enforcing standards and procedures to screen and identify TANF recipients with a history of domestic violence, will refer such individuals to counseling and supportive services, and will provide "good cause" waivers of normal program requirements when compliance world make it more difficult to escape domestic violence or unfairly penalize them. The FVO waivered cases still would count in the calculation of the state's work participation rate, but if their inclusion causes the rate to fall short of requirements, the state may receive penalty relief on grounds of having had reasonable cause for the failure. Similarly, the 60-month federal time limit clock does not stop for waivered cases, but in their time limit can be extended; and if the result is that extensions exceed the 20% hardship allowance, the state may receive penalty relief. To receive federal recognition, good cause domestic violence waivers must meet certain standards.

State Actions

As of mid-May, 2000, all 54 TANF jurisdictions except 11 (Connecticut, Indiana, Maine, Michigan, Ohio, South Dakota, Vermont, the Virgin Islands, Virginia, Wisconsin, and Wyoming) had adopted the FVO. Indiana said that it already exempted domestic violence victims from employment and training, child support, and time limit requirements; and that it would adopt the FVO once it expanded the domestic violence service infrastructure sufficiently to comply with federal rules. In late November 2001, the state said it hoped to accomplish this by July 1, 2002.

Among the states with FVO certification, there is great variation in domestic violence victim notification and screening procedures, state-wideness, service delivery by professionals trained in domestic violence, waivers of requirements, and length of waiver. Some of the states choosing not to certify for the FVO, including Connecticut, Michigan, and Wisconsin, have procedures in effect to identify and serve victims of domestic abuse. In its 2000 state TANF report, Wisconsin said case managers work closely with domestic violence victims and that the state's strategy is supported by the Wisconsin Coalition Against Domestic Violence, which as helped the state develop staff training. Wisconsin also said it considered it counterproductive to categorically waive program rules because in the past persons exempted from work rules often had received no services. In first annual state TANF reports (for FY2000), California estimated that it granted 2,042 good cause waivers under FVO in FY2000, New York said it gave 4,755 waivers during CY1999, and one state (Pennsylvania) and most of its waivers concerned child support cooperation, not work rules. Kansas reported that domestic violence issues were disclosed by 4.6 percent of TRANF applicants/recipients (248 out of 5,330) who received information about domestic violence services and were screened in the Topeka office by an "on-site advocate." Of these, 14 were determined to need a domestic violence waiver.

Legislation

The Leave No Child Behind Act, *S. 940/H.R. 1990*, would require state programs of unemployment compensation to cover persons who lose their jobs because of domestic violence. It also would authorize grants for research on the impact of domestic violence on children. Another bill, *H.R. 2258*, would exempt certain persons who suffer from domestic abuse from a general citizenship requirement for eligibility for major welfare programs. *S. 1249/H.R. 2670* would entitle victims of domestic and sexual violence of emergency leave for medical or legal help, counseling, safety planning, and other remedies. It would allow use of TANF funds for short-term emergency payments to any person taking this leave. Since enactment of TANF, the Senate has twice voted to forbid any numerical limit on TANF time-limit hardship exemptions for domestic violence victims, but the House has not agreed. Most recently, the Battered Women's Economic Security and Safety Act of 1999, S. 1069 (106th Congress), proposed to prohibit numerical limits on time limit hardship exemptions for persons with domestic violence waivers and to exclude waivered individuals from the calculation of state work participation rates.

Chapter 7

WELFARE LAW AND DOMESTIC VIOLENCE

Jacqueline Cooke and Vee Burke

SUMMARY

The Family Violence Option (FVO) of the 1996 welfare law (P.L. 104-193) permits state programs of Temporary Assistance for Needy Families (TANF) to waive federal rules regarding required work, time limited benefits, and child support cooperation for victims of domestic violence. The purpose of the FVO is to enable states to help victims of domestic violence without subjecting them to TANF rules that might "unfairly penalize" them or put them at further risk of abuse. Out of 54 jurisdictions with TANF programs, 44 have adopted the FVO. In the first annual state TANF reports, California estimated that it granted 2,042 good cause waivers under FVO in FY2000, New York said it gave 4,755 waivers during CY1999, and one state (Pennsylvania) said most of its waivers concerned child support cooperation, not work rules. However, most states provided no waiver data. This chapter details the history, implementation and implications of the FVO.

INTRODUCTION

The 1996 welfare law (P.L. 104-193) replaced the entitlement program of Aid to Families with Dependent Children (AFDC) and other related programs with the block grant program of Temporary Assistance to Needy Families (TANF). To receive their full share of federal funding, states must enforce some federal requirements on parents: minimum work participation rates, a 60-montyh time limit on federally-funded benefits, and cooperation in child support enforcement.[1]

Federal statute does not provide for any automatic exemption of individuals from program requirements but does enable states to extend the 60-month benefit cutoff for 20% of the state's caseload on grounds of "hardship" or the family's inclusion of an individual who has been battered or subjected to extreme cruelty. Individuals who have a history of domestic violence can be classified by the state as hardship cases within the 20% cap. In addition, a provision called the Family Violence Option (FVO) allows states to exempt qualifying victims of domestic violence from any TANF rule. States that certify that they have adopted the FVO have a greater capacity to exempt other "hardship" cases from the time limit without risk of penalty.

FAMILY VIOLENCE OPTION

The Family Violence Option is an *optional* certification in a state TANF plan, specifying that the state has established and is enforcing standards and procedures to screen and identify TANF recipients with a history of domestic violence, will refer such individuals to counseling and supportive services, and will provide "good cause" waivers of normal program requirements when compliance would make it more difficult to escape domestic violence or unfairly penalize them. The FVO provision defines

---

[1] Failure by a state to achieve the required work participation rate is to result in a decrease in funding of 5% for the first year of noncompliance, increasing by 2% for each subsequent year that compliance is not achieved, not to exceed 21%. The penalty may be reduced based on the severity of noncompliance or if noncompliance is due to extraordinary circumstances such as a nature disaster or regional recession. Penalty for violating the 60-month time limit is a 5% decrease in federal funds. If a state is not enforcing penalties against individuals who fail to cooperate in procedures to enforce child support orders, federal funding is to be decreased by not more than 5%. However, none of these penalties may be imposed if the state is determined to have reasonable cause for noncompliance. (Section 409(b)(2) of the Social Security Act).

"domestic violence" as having the same meaning as the term "battered or subject to extreme cruelty" in the time-limit hardship language.[2]

For persons with a history of domestic violence or who are at risk of further violence, the FVO allows states to waive program requirements. If a state that has granted good cause domestic violence waivers under the FVO fails to meet the minimum work participation rate, but they are eligible for removal from calculation of penalties. The state also will not be penalized for failure to enforce child support cooperation if enforcement would put the victim at risk of further abuse.

States with FVO certification can give time limit extensions above the 20% hardship cap to families that have federally recognized good cause domestic violence waivers. The 60-month federal time limit clock does not stop despite these waivers, but the time limit can be extended for so long as necessary without penalty. Families that have received ongoing cash assistance through a state TANF program since July, 1997, mandatory start date for TANK, will lose federal cash assistance in July, 2002 unless they are extended by the state under the 20% hardship cap or have been granted a good cause domestic violence waiver. (In the many states that began TANF before the deadline, the time limit will be reached earlier than July 2002.)

For federal recognition of good cause domestic violence waivers, the state must provide: 1) individualized responses and services strategies consistent with the needs of individual victims; 2) *temporary* waivers (not to exceed 6 months); and 3) in lieu of program requirements, alternative services for victims consistent with individualized responses and service strategies. Waivers are available only to individuals in states that have adopted the FVO in their state plan. Outside of the state plan, states also can request approval from the Department of Health and Services (HHS) for FVO certification in corrective action plans, which are submitted by states that have failed to meet federal requirements. This procedure is to deter states from using the FVO as a "quick fix" to avoid penalties instead of as a broad strategy to best serve victims of domestic abuse.

States also must comply with a reporting rule to gain federal recognition of good cause domestic violence waivers. In an annual report, first required for FY2000 of states requesting recognition of good cause domestic violence waivers, states must provide a description of the strategies and procedures in

---

[2] Section 408 (a)(7)(iii) of the Social Security Act defines battered or subject to extreme cruelty as having been subjected to physical acts that resulted in, or threatened to result in, physical injury to the individual; sexual abuse; sexual activity involving a dependent child; being forced as the caretaker relative of a dependent child to engage in nonconsensual sexual acts or activiti4es; threats of, or attempts at, physical or sexual abuse; mental abuse; or neglect or deprivation of medical care.

place to service victims of domestic violence and the aggregate number of good cause domestic violence waivers granted.

Recipients with waived program requirements under the FVO can receive assistance indefinitely, subject to redetermination at least every 6 months. Each recipient must have an appropriate services plan that is developed by a person trained in domestic violence, reflects individualized assessment and is designed to lead to work. The development of an appropriate services plan by a trained professional requires that state TANF programs train staff in domestic violence or coordinate with an agency/organization for assistance in developing individualized plans.

STATE IMPLEMENTATION OF FVO

As of mid-May, 2001, all TANF jurisdictions except ten (Connecticut, Maine, Michigan, Ohio, South Dakota, Vermont, the Virgin Islands, Virginia, Wisconsin, and Wyoming) had adopted the FVO. Illinois was the most recent state to take the option; in March, after the Illinois House voted unanimously to require the state human services department to adopt the option, the department said it would do so administratively.

Among the states with FVO certification, there is great variation in procedures to notification and screening, statewideness, service delivery by professionals trained in domestic violence, waivers of requirements, and length of waiver. States also vary in how they inform recipients of the domestic violence good cause waiver. Some inform recipients orally, encouraging the recipient's oral disclosure of an abusive situation or history; others rely on questions on application forms and/or supplemental brochures and pamphlets. The different procedures could affect which recipients are notified and how willing a victim is to disclose her history.

As is consistent with the devolution of many state TANF programs, a state that has adopted the FVO is not mandated to have statewide implementation. Colorado has certified adoption of the FVO but defers to each county the option to adopt FVO compliant procedures. Many states defer service development and implementation of domestic violence services to the counties under standards set by the state. Most states grant waivers on a case-by-case basis so there is great flexibility for the caseworker to either deny or pursue a good cause waiver.

In complying with the FVO requirement for development of an appropriate services plan by a trained professional, some states have provided training for caseworkers within the welfare agency. Others have chosen to have the welfare agency to coordinate with another agency or organization to develop a plan. (The state of Kansas defines staff who have received training designed by the Kansas Coalition Against Domestic Violence and Sexual Abuse as "persons trained in domestic violence.")

States determine which requirements to waive on an individual basis as part of the victims services plan. One state (Maryland) effectively stops the federal time clock for victims by assisting them with state funds until the barriers caused by domestic violence have been removed. Since domestic violence victims in Maryland are moved into a separate state program, they are not subject to federal rules, and states cannot be penalized for any exemption made for individuals assisted by a state-funded program. For domestic violence victims in federally funded TANF programs, the federal clock continues to tick.[3] FVO waivers are the only way that domestic violence victims can be assured ongoing federal cash aid after the 60-month time limit, unless the state includes them under the 20% "hardship" exception.

Federal regulations limit waivers to no longer than six months, subject to redetermination. Most states provide waivers indefinitely, subject to biannual redetermination. These two redeterminations usually assess compliance with the individual's services plan as an indication of progress and grounds for an extended waiver. Some states limit the length of a waiver of certain requirements. For example, Minnesota exempts domestic violence victims from employment requirements for a lifetime maximum of 12 months. Montana provides an exemption to its state time limit for up to six months. Texas allows waiver of limits, child support cooperation, and work requirements for up to one year.

Some other states choosing not to certify for the FVO, including Connecticut, Michigan, and Wisconsin, have procedures in effect to identify and serve the victims of domestic abuse. In its 2000 state TANF report, Wisconsin said case managers work closely with domestic violence victims and that the state's strategy is supported by the Wisconsin Coalition Against Domestic Violence, which has helped the state develop staff training. Wisconsin also said it considered it counterproductive to categorically waive program rules because in the past persons exempted from work rules often had received no services. In Ohio, County departments have the responsibility for devising policy about cooperation and assessment of domestic violence.

---

[3] Many states have set benefit cutoff time limits shorter than 60 months, and some of them stop their state clocks for victims of domestic violence; some others to do not stop the state clock but provide extensions once the time limit is reached.

DATA ON WAIVERS

Initial annual state TANF reports (for FY2000) provide these data on good cause waivers granted under the FVO: Arizona, 167; California, 2042; Colorado, none; Delaware, none; Kansas, 14; Kentucky 329; Maryland, 98; Minnesota, 635; Montana, none from work rules; New Mexico, 9; New York, 4,755 in CY1999; Pennsylvania, 320 as of December 30, 2000 (223 from child support rules, 97 from work rules); Puerto Rico; 20 from child for rules, not from work rules; South Carolina, 27; and Texas, 195. Florida said that although it granted no waivers, it gave domestic violence "deferrals" from work activity in 755 cases for a limited time (while alternate activity plans were developed). Louisiana and Missouri said they were unable to provide the data, but Missouri said it would provide data for the next report. Oregon, which gave no data, said that for reasons of client safety, it had not created an identifier on the computer to track FVO waivers. Tennessee, which reported no data, said that it imposed strict "confidentiality boundaries" between the domestic violence counselor and the eligibility counselor and that the latter was not always aware of the cause of a waiver.

HISTORY OF THE FAMILY VIOLENCE OPTION

The Family Violence Option was enacted as part of the 1996 welfare reform law (P.L. 104-193). The concept behind the FVO can be traced back to a 1995 Wellstone-Murray amendment to H.R. 4, a version of TANF that was vetoed. The amendment would have *required* states to adopt the FVO and *excluded* domestic violence victims with waivers from the calculation of state work participation rates. This provision passed in the Senate but was rejected by the House. Senator of Wellstone proposed a similar amendment, calling for mandatory state certification, in the 1996 legislation leading to the P.L. 104-193. The amendment passed in the Senate but was not included in the House version of the bill that the Senate subsequently adopted. Since FVO enactment in 1996, the Senate has twice passed a bill to forbid any numerical limit on time-limit hardship exemptions for domestic violence in victims, but the House has not followed suit. Representative Schumer proposed bills twice (1996 and 1997) to require state certification of the FVO (H.R. 4324, H.R. 2861), and the Battered Women's Economic Security and Safety Act of 1999, S. 1069, proposed to prohibit numerical limits on time-limit hardship exemptions for persons with domestic violence waivers under the FVO and to exclude waivered individuals from the calculation of state to work participation rates.

INCIDENCE OF DOMESTIC VIOLENCE AND EFFECT ON EMPLOYMENT

Numerous studies have attempted to document the prevalence of domestic violence and implications on employment for welfare families. Conferees on P.L. 105-33 directed the General Account Office (GAO) to submit a report on the impact of domestic violence on the use of welfare. The GAO conducted and analysis of past studies of welfare recipients and found that between 15 percent and 56 percent of the women surveyed reported that they were or had been victims of physical domestic abuse in the twelve months preceding the survey and that 55 percent to 65 percent had been physically abused by intimate partner at some point in their lives.[4]

The GAO report could not conclude that domestic violence affected the victim's likelihood of work. No study could isolate the effects of domestic violence on employment status. A 1997 Massachusetts study of AFDC recipients found similar employment rates for women who reported having been abused or not (8.8 % and 7%, respectively). However, a study of women in a low-income neighborhood in Chicago found that women reported to have been subject to abuse at some point suffered more spells of unemployment, greater job turnover, and significantly higher rates of receipt of AFDC, Medicaid and food stamps. The GAO report said that women who currently experience domestic violence may differ in their ability to obtain and maintain employment from the women who have safely escaped from past violence.

The GAO review suggests that of users may hinder their victims from obtaining and maintaining employment. Abusers often feel threatened by women's best efforts toward self-sufficiency that might afford them the option to leave the abusive relationship. Between 16 % and 60 % of the women surveyed in five studies reported that their partner had discouraged them from working, and 33 % to 46 % said their partner prevented them from working. Abusive partners often attempt to sabotage women's work efforts by becoming violent, promising childcare and then failing to deliver, destroying or hiding items needed for women's work activities, harassing

---

[4] General Accounting Office. *Domestic Violence: prevalence Backup and Implications for Employment Among on Welfare Recipients.* GAO/HEHS-99-12. November 1998.

them at their work site by phone or in person, and inflict invisible signs of abuse that women will be too embarrassed to attend their work activity. Three studies found that 44% to 60% of respondents have been reprimanded at work for behaviors caused by the abusive situation, and 24% to 52% said they lost their jobs as a result of abuse. Further, domestic violence inflicts physical and emotional health problems on women that can affect their ability to find and maintain employment. Studies show that victims of domestic violence suffer from chronic health problems, low self-esteem, greater anxiety and anger than nonabused women, depression and post-traumatic stress disorder.

IMPLICATIONS OF THE FVO

Although most states have certified in their adoption of the FVO, many may not need federally recognized good cause domestic violence waivers to escape fiscal penalties for time-limit or were participation failures. This is because many states appear unlikely to exceed the 20% hardship cap on time-limit extensions or to fail work participation rates, which has been sharply lowered because of caseload reduction. However, because of the sharp decline in caseload, fewer individuals can be exempted under the 20% hardship cap.

When states to request federal recognition of waivers, their reporting of domestic violence need not be comprehensive. States are required only to describe the standards and procedures they have established and the number of waivers for which they seek federal recognition under the FVO. Domestic violence victims may be exempt from work requirements through another category, such as having to care for a young child or handicapped relative. They may also benefit through access to domestic violence services, although not given an exemption from any welfare rule. Some states are developing databases that can track the number of welfare assistance applicants disclosing past or current domestic abuse, the number requesting waivers and the number of waivers granted. These numbers will provide a more complete picture of the prevalence of domestic violence among recipients and the assistance states provide them.

INDEX